Daddy

Can I Tell You Something

Black Daughters Speak To Their Fathers

EDITED BY
ANGELA FLOYD

Daddy,
Can I Tell You Something?

Black Daughters Speak To Their Fathers

Edited by Angela Floyd

SELA PRESS   COLLEGE PARK, MD

First Printing 2006

ISBN 0-9761310-0-5

Cover and book design by Michael Fleishman

Printed in the U.S.A.

For us.

I am because we are,
and because we are,
therefore,
I am.
—African Proverb

I would like to thank my family: my husband, Frederick Iverson; my wonderful daughters, Safeeyah, Zion and Sela; my mothers, Agnes Floyd, Deborah Iverson, Eva Belle Mathis and Juanita Wasson; my sisters, Laura, Lisa, Linda, Jenifer, Julie and Mary; and my brothers, Vincent, Lance and Mark. Thanks to friends for your advice and support: Antionette Sweet, Martrice Lumpkin, Vanessa Roberts, Crystal Jones, Nancy Brown, Amy Lloyd, Jackie Walker, Lisa Rosenthal, Renee Catacalos and Victor LaValle. Special thanks to my fabulous technicians: Nestor Hernandez, Marcia Davis, Michael Fleishman, Leena Jayaswal and Ernest Floyd.

Thanks, Dad. For everything.

Last, but definitely not least, thank you to all of you who shared your stories. Without your bravery, there would be no book.

Contents

I. Where You Been At, Daddy?

II. Daddy, Thank You

III. *How Could You Hurt Me, Daddy?*

IV. *Do You Rest In Peace, Daddy?*

Introduction

I am the last of ten children born to James and Agnes Floyd. I was born and raised in the inner city of Cleveland, Ohio. My father worked as a maintenance man. My mother earned her bachelor's degree in education but gave up her teaching career to stay at home and raise her children.

Raising ten children on a maintenance man's salary meant that we were poor by any standard, and we certainly faced all of the inherent dangers and potential pitfalls of growing up in the inner city. My parents, however, held us to the highest of standards. They put a premium on education, hard work, spirituality and character. My mother was struck with rheumatoid arthritis when I was born and deteriorated physically from there, but she faced everyday willing to do whatever it took to provide us with a stable home. My father, my dear father, unable to afford a car, rode two buses across town to work in one of the city's worst housing projects every morning and every evening until the year he died at age 72.

I consider my life and work a tribute to my parents' love, sacrifices and indomitable spirits. The woman that I have become, the wife, mother, friend and professional that I have become, I attribute largely to my father. He was there and that comfort, that stability, was mine, no matter what I had to face outside our home.

Daddy, Can I Tell You Something?

Having my father in the home and engaged in my life was all I knew, but our relationship was extraordinary compared with other girls my age in my neighborhood. Most of the girls I knew had estranged relationships with their fathers, but my father was at home everyday caring for our family. He showed me manhood without any contradictions.

My father died of lung cancer when I was 17 years old. I was too destroyed to grieve, too numb. I was too worn from the harshness of the eight months of sickness and dying to process the actual death. I just kept moving, but eventually things caught up with me. I became a mother, and my husband and my little girl became a father and daughter right there before me, throwing it in my face with every kiss, hug, smile, dance, game. Showing me that I was incomplete. I was a daughter with no father, a girl without a man to love her unconditionally, the way my father loved me, the way my husband loved my daughter. The finality of my father's death hit me, and I began to grieve hard.

I confided in a friend and her response was, "At least you had him." Her response enraged me, and I argued that she didn't understand, but she insisted, "You had him. You have memories that actually happened. I am grieving over someone, something I only imagined. I mourn a ghost. I make up things. I don't have a father, never had one, and will never have one." I didn't know what to say. We cried together for our losses.

After that, I couldn't stop thinking about her. I started talking to other friends about their fathers. Some could not and would not talk about their fathers, some could not stop talking. What really struck me was that, without exception, whether they were willing to talk about their fathers or not, all of these women had extremely intense feelings about their relationship with their fathers.

I had so many thoughts and so many questions, and so did the women I spoke to. Why do we crave our fathers so much, whether we see him everyday, from time to time, or never? Why do most of us carry around the effects of our relationship with him for our entire lives? And what is the impact, the cost, of our emotional and spiritual fixation with this relationship?

I placed an ad in Poets & Writers magazine requesting submissions for a book about Black fathers and daughters. Then, I contacted Essence magazine. I told them about the book. I let them know that I had very little money but that the book was important, and an ad in their magazine could help us reach thousands of women. They agreed. They gave me a paragraph in the back of the magazine. I put other requests for submissions online. I also gave fliers to everybody I knew in as many cities as I could cover and told them to post them everywhere.

I ended up with a huge pile of submissions. I had to figure out how to approach the pieces. I wanted a broad array of women speaking candidly about their lives without the veil of politics or psycho-social babble. I wanted raw voices, voices I hadn't heard before. I wanted to feel what I felt when I heard women like Janie Crawford, Celie, Polly Breedlove, Precious Jones, and Ursa Corregidora tell their stories. We knew when we read their stories that we were reading about parts of our lives that had gone ignored and untold for too long.

I decided that the best approach was to just start reading the submissions I received and that is what I did until something started bothering me. I received pieces about good fathers, but only a few compared to the stacks of essays, short stories, letters and poems about bad relationships. While I started the book with an eye towards confronting and dealing with pain I knew I was going to encounter, including my own, I was overwhelmed by the magnitude of the suffering. I felt that I had turned on a faucet and couldn't turn it off. The sadness was flooding my office, my apartment, my life. From 8 to 90 years old, daughters were struggling with father issues. No matter the age or socioeconomic background of the women, the bottom line was the same over and over and over again: profound pain and suffering.

I didn't know what to do. I cried, stepped away, came back, prayed, meditated, and prayed some more. I didn't know what to do with the sexual, physical and emotional abuse so many women had endured at the hands of their own fathers. I didn't know what to do with the childlike voices, and sometimes childlike writing, of grown women asking, "Where were you?" "Why didn't you protect me?" "Why did you hurt me?" "Why were you so mean?" "Why did you die and leave me?" Often where I expected anger from the daughters, I got love and forgiveness, including instances of sexual abuse. I didn't know what to do with my own pain and grief when a woman nearly killed me with her story of losing her treasured father to cancer. She was singing my song.

I thought that I had taken on too much. I thought about ending the project, but I couldn't. Not after all of these women had been brave enough to write. So, although I felt extremely unsteady, I was determined to finish what I started.

I put off going through all the submissions. I selected a few pieces, works portraying a range of father-daughter relationships. I edited them quickly and sent them out to agents. Several responded. They liked the idea of the book, but they wanted it to have more mass appeal. They suggested adding some "star power."

I was already off-balance from the emotional weight of the project, so I got busy looking for friends of friends who could connect me with celebrities with father-daughter issues. And I found a few. But I realized that I didn't want that kind of book. Celebrities were not part of my vision, even if they would sell more books.

I stopped dealing with agents. I decided to edit, publish, and market the book in-house. In my house, to be exact. Whatever came to pass would come to pass, but I would know that I followed my heart. So I got to work. It took years, but, with the help of friends, we reviewed every single piece submitted.

After I read and reread these submissions, I tried to categorize them. An old issue reared up again: the book was unbalanced. There were too few stories about healthy father-daughter relationships and too many stories about absent or otherwise unavailable dads. Where were my good dads?

I knew that most of the women I knew didn't have relationships with their fathers, but I couldn't believe that what I was seeing was right. I made a list of all the women I knew and counted the ones who were raised by their fathers. The numbers looked bad. So bad that I went out in the streets and started asking every Black woman I saw if she had been raised by her father. Again, I came up short, real short. I had no intention of publishing a book portraying all Black men as irresponsible, violent, no-count fathers, but I also wasn't going to ignore or diminish the scope of the problem.

This book raised real questions. When did so many men stop defining themselves by what they contribute to their family and community? When did so many men disconnect the measure of their manhood from their measure as fathers? If too many Black men are, or end up, on drugs, in jail, self-destructive and perversely misogynistic, what has and will become of their children? If too many Black women are damaged from their experiences with their own fathers and subsequent relationships with men, how can they live healthy lives and raise healthy children?

I don't know the answers. All I can do is what I set out to do: let the daughters speak, uncensored. The questions and the answers are in the stories.

The first section of the book focuses on absent fathers. Some of these daughters have never met their fathers while others remember fathers whose presence was devastatingly sporadic and rare. Still others painfully recall the day their father left home, and, for most, never returned. These stories share the pain of not having a father in the home, and the feelings of rejection, lovelessness and mistrust that stemmed from his absence.

In the second section, daughters express gratitude for fathers who played a positive role in their daughters' lives. This section reveals sides of Black men that are rarely seen or spoken of: Daddy cooking in the kitchen, oiling hair, working, gardening. Some of these fathers even raised their daughters alone, a wonderful testament to Black fatherhood.

The third section features the stories of daughters who experienced verbal, physical or sexual abuse at their fathers' hands. This section also includes women scarred by the presence of emotionally distant fathers. Some have reached a place of forgiveness that has allowed them to love their fathers in spite of their actions while others are still angry and struggling to heal.

The final section focuses on the experience of losing a father to death. Some women pay tribute to their fathers; others lament that he ever existed. Death has left these daughters to grapple alone with their feelings. Death has ended whatever conversation they could have had with their fathers.

Daughters, whatever our issues, we are not alone. Fathers, whatever your issues, you are not alone. Let's read together, laugh together, cry together, grieve together, get mad together, pray together, and begin our healing.

Together.

With the blessings of our ancestors, let us begin.

Angela Floyd

Our Fathers

they live
because of us
in spite of us

they die
as men
as boys

they rest
in peace
in pieces

they come back
like guards
like thieves

we are their daughters
swollen with their stories

Angela Floyd

I. Where You Been At, Daddy?

Stealing Fathers

Danielle Iverson

It was a cold day in October when the million men marched. They were marching like soldiers on Washington to the beat of atonement. They were all in step, marching to become better husbands to the women who loved them, better dads to the children they fathered and better men for their own sakes.

I sat in my living room watching the marchers on television and living through them. I laughed when they laughed, shouted amen when they shouted amen and cried when they cried. I looked for my father even though I knew he wasn't among them.

I had saved the child support checks that I received every two weeks. Six checks later, I had enough money to support my father on his journey to Washington, DC. When I sent him the money and information about the Million Man March, he returned it to me with a note about too many niggas, too much walking, too much money to be lost at work just to go to DC. Oh, and that he loved me, his beautiful Black princess.

When my father was eighteen, he gathered all that he was in his arms and carefully spread it out on a table. A grizzled-looking white man surveyed the pieces of my father's life with cold gray eyes. The man's withered hands handled and examined what had been put before him. Then, he pointed at my father, a street boy with thick muscles covered in the blackest of skin, and said, "Welcome to the United States Marine Corps, Son." He erased my father's name, his smile, his friends, his family, his woman, his passions, his boyhood, his son, and his dreams. When the last trace of Frederick David Iverson was gone, the man labeled him: Property of the U.S. Marine Corps. Vietnam.

When he received his letter of induction, my father framed it. He hung it on the cracked beige wall like a college diploma, something he would never earn. On the same wall, a small clock counted down the time my father had left until he went to boot camp. My mother, sixteen then, cradled my father's namesake in her arms. She cried as she watched the clock and felt the baby's tiny lips on her breast.

I often wonder if my father, with his new wife and new baby, ever regretted enlisting for the war. Did he ever look at that letter framed so nicely on the peeling wall and wonder if he could place it in an envelope with a letter saying he had changed his mind? Second thoughts didn't matter, though. He went into the military and on to Vietnam. He was not like friends who suddenly acquired odd limps or coke-bottle eyeglasses. He left behind others, too, men with manicured hands and lawns who had never lifted anything heavier than a pencil. They were shielded from war by their upper-class status. College students my father's age breathed sighs of relief when they received their letters of deferment. They carried books in one hand and signs protesting the war in the other. Later, they would boast how they courageously served on the front lines protesting the war at home. My father, on the other hand, who never pretended, would be silenced by his memories of the jungles of Vietnam.

Sometimes, I wish that he would have purposely flunked the tests that landed him in the Marines. If I could have, I would have urged him to walk with a ridiculous limp. I wish he would have pretended to be ignorant and, although his pride would have been hurt, he could have gone home to his family. But my father was an honest man, and it was honest men like my father who left behind namesakes to ensure that their memories lived on just in case they never returned. It was honest men like my father who could not stand to appear anything less than brave in the eyes of their women, even though they were scared inside.

I don't know about the things that my father collected in Vietnam. I wish I did. There are times when I want him to unlock the door between us and let me in. The door, though, has remained bolted, and I stand outside piecing together scraps of information about Vietnam, about my father. I am left to create the images.

I see my father in his fatigues, hiding in the lush green of a place unfamiliar and foreign. He is looking straight ahead even though his thoughts drift back to the family he has left behind. He is thinking of how he can survive and make it home. He does what he has to do. As if stepping out of himself, he sheds his skin and leaves it by the way side.

Everything about him changes. The softness in his eyes becomes a hard glint. His jaw tightens, locking itself. And as his hands grip the black steel of his rifle, he stops thinking about home because to get home, to survive, he must let it all go.

My father returned from Vietnam with medals for his bravery. But now it was home that was unfamiliar and foreign. When he tried to shed his skin for a second time, he found that he could not. The hard glint in his eyes remained. So did the tightness in his jaw.

Daddy, Can I Tell You Something?

Even now, he seldom smiles and laughter rarely escapes his lips.

He returned home a stranger, unrecognizable to his family and even to himself. He came back to my mother and my brother. Later, my sister was born, and, still later, I was born. My mother and father divorced when I was six months old. Because of this I have no memories or stories of my own to tell about my father and me. I see him sometimes, but I don't know him at all.

So, I steal. I snatch other peoples' memories of their fathers and make them my own. I have been the little girl whose father checks under her bed and inside the closet before she goes to sleep to make sure that the Bogeyman isn't there. I once was the little girl whose father held her up almost to the sky, so that she could slam dunk on a kid's basketball hoop. And I have been the girl whose father watches her from the stands with pride in his eyes as his favorite basketball star runs the floor like a pro.

In reality, I am a girl who looks in the mirror every morning and curses my reflection. People say, "That girl sho' do look like Fred spit her right out." It is too painful to resemble someone I love but don't like. On the other hand, my father is proud of the person he has made. There has never been a time when I have seen him, and he has not commented on how "beautiful" I am. Although I accept his superficial compliments, I contemplate marring my cheeks like tribal decoration to show him how much I dislike the features I have inherited from him. I am a girl who hopes every year that my father will call me on my birthday. Every year, I have waited in vain.

My father's marching in Vietnam led him away from me. I wanted the Million Man March to be about him returning to me. The longer I watched it on television, the harder I wept. I was happy to see all those Black men united, but the tears I cried were for me, as I could only pretend that one of those men was my Dad marching to become a better father to me.

Flying East

Sheba White

Dear James,

Moms told me once, because I must have asked, that you only had one leg. One leg was gone. Gone? Gone where? I asked about your missing leg. It was easier than asking about why you were missing. Where had your leg gone? Had it had gotten tired of holding you up and simply walked away? Your yellow leg leaving you behind. I could only imagine what you looked like. You were like Barbie missing limbs, with her hair half-shaved, half-wild with over-braiding, dyed by leftover Dark & Lovely. For years, this is how I knew you and dreamed of you, broken and mangled.

There was never a picture I could run the tips of my fingers over, a profile to study. There was never a gruff chin to lean into. Never musky skin and whiskey breath in a midnight kiss to stir me from sleep. Moms said, "Yellow, low life, shiftless, 'scuse my French, asshole thinks he's gonna—." But, besides the missing leg, that was all she ever gave of you. No address, no name, no history.

I loved you, though, always. I loved you even before I found the letter you sent years ago from Vietnam. It said "Dear M____, Tell my daughter I love her and that I hope I do not die here." I squeezed it into the palm of my hand and read it until the black letters curled hieroglyphic. I rung the letter through my teeth to see if I could taste your sweat, your fear. You had lost your leg, you wrote. I tried to feel you.

I saw you only once, ten or twelve years ago. Moms was pulling me along fast, her long legs in full stride. Her calves were bony, her thighs big, like upside down somethings. She was mad that day. Her "why I gots to—" floated through the air. I didn't care though, I was counting down like in the movies when something exciting is about to happen or something is about to explode.

We flew like black birds through the heaving sky, west to east, to see you. I loved flying, the clouds were thick and comforting. By the time we landed in Newark and two-stepped across Manhattan, I had forgotten why we had come. Until we got to you. You saw me and said, "What have they been feeding you up there?" I saw you, and my heart wilted. You were too old, you were gnarled on a barstool, your eyes were muddy, your breath smelled of beer and one of your legs was really missing. You never touched me. But you were mine, my Jesus, my breath.

In a sea of people I could not find you. I have a vague recollection of you, the old man with one leg. Or sometimes I imagine you a leather-clad insect, the leather grasshopper with fighter pilot goggles because I heard you rode motorcycles. I don't know where I got that from, but it was something to have. Where were you, Daddy?

Later, Mom and I fly East again. I find out on this ride that you, with a bullet searing through the soft tissue of your cranium, died fast. Died alone in some drunken brawl about manhood and money, and I am angry. Because not only were you not there, you were gone before I could find you, pin you down and make you give yourself to me and make you take me as yours, all of me—my thick legs, my small breasts, my flat nose, my strong teeth, my flat feet. All of me.

Your daughter, Sheba

Fly Daddy's Angel, Fly

Deidre L. Shannon

"Did he see us?" my sister asked.

"I don't know. Keep driving," I said.

I wanted to look, to see his face. But if I did, my sister would know that I still loved him and that would disgust her. He looked so alone standing there in winter's embrace, his daughters driving away from him without a glance. Seeing him, nostalgia stole me back home to New Orleans.

I was at the white house in the middle of the block, where my sisters and I played double dutch and the boys played touch football in the street. That was the only house we ever owned, and it was the first time we had brand new carpet. The day we moved in, I raced straight for the room I had decided was going to be mine. I sat on the floor and ran my fingers through the carpet. It felt like Daddy's hair. I pulled off my shoe to feel the brown plushness between my toes. I ran around the room dragging the feeling beneath my feet. I was laughing hysterically.

I finally stopped, but the room continued to spin. A sick feeling rose in my throat. Static electricity raced through my body. I reached for something to hold me up, but I shocked myself and fell to the floor. I sat there, head spinning, smiling and thinking how worth it the nausea, dizziness and electric shock were for our new carpet in our new house.

The ticking of the car blinker brought me back.

"This isn't the turn," I said. I glanced in the rear view mirror. He was still standing there. That was the last time I saw my father. For a second, I felt carpet between my toes.

I called him Poppy, and he meant everything to me. I will never forget the day he crowned me a princess. I was eight years old.

"When I was a young man," he said, "I prayed to Allah everyday, and I asked Him for a beautiful, dark-skinned, intelligent daughter. Allah heard my prayer and sent you to me. Don't tell anyone else, but you are my most precious child. You are my Black angel."

The words filled me up. I held that secret so close to my heart there wasn't much room for anything else. At that moment, I knew that I had been placed upon a pedestal by the man I loved more than any other. I thought nothing could ever tear us apart. Then, he left. My father, my pedestal, my faith. Gone.

My mother brought the news to me. She came into the bedroom I shared with my sister, and I knew something was wrong. She looked tired, defeated. She told us to sit down. She said that she had something to tell us. I stood. Her lips began to move. All I heard were her first few words explaining what was wrong between her and Poppy. My heart stopped beating. Silence engulfed me, deafened me. I ran. I ran until I passed out in the middle of the kitchen floor.

Daddy, Can I Tell You Something?

I woke up in my mother's bed. My eyes were swollen from crying. My Poppy? How could he do the things Mommy said he did? And how could he leave us? He was my father. Didn't they understand? He was my father.

Years later, while out jogging one morning, I saw him driving to work. I watched as he drove past without looking back at me, and I cried. I cried because even with the pain of feeling betrayed, I still loved my Poppy. And I hated him. I hated him for leaving. I hated him for building my pedestal only to rip it out from under me. This hate reverberated through all my relationships. As much as I wanted to, I just couldn't seem to let love be love. Love scared me. Trusting scared me.

I began crying the day I found out that my Poppy was leaving, and I never stopped. Then I got tired of feeling beaten and weak. I prayed to God to help me, to heal me. Something inside of me was dead, and I wanted it to be alive again. I cried, and I prayed for years.

There are still days that I wonder about him. I guess I forgive him. I may even still love him. But more important, I understand that I don't need him to be complete. I am complete in God.

The last time I went home to that same room where once I spun until I was dizzy, the carpet was gone. There was nothing there but cold, hardwood floors.

Before I Met My Father

Crystal E. Wilkinson

All the years before I met my father, he was who I needed him to be. When I was seven, maybe eight, he worked in a candy factory and brought me as many Redhots, Now and Laters, Lemonheads and Laffy Taffy as I wanted. When I was ten, he made Barbie dolls. At fourteen, I said he was a roadie with the Jackson Five. But nobody in Middleburg had ever seen my father. Truth was, I had never seen him either. Didn't even know his name until I was fifteen.

In 1978, my mother and I lived with my grandparents right outside Middleburg on Route 198. My mother was trying to recover from a breakdown and any word about my father was cursed.

My mother was a true-d yo-yo. On her down days, I took the long way around her chair so as not to walk in front of the TV when her stories were on. She eyed me like a bobcat, waiting for one fuck-up. I played quiet mouse, imagining myself walking on clouds or cotton balls. I fed myself, warming up a can of ravioli or

21

beanie weenies or eating corn flakes or Vienna sausage, always careful not to clang my spoon against the bowl or to rattle the dishes into the sink until my grandmother came home. On her up days, we held hands, window shopped at the dime store over in Liberty, or jumped in my grandfather's old LTD and headed up to the farm so we could wade in the creek or swim. At home we played hopscotch and fixed fried apple pies. She kissed me on the lips like only a mother could and smiled so wide that I could have counted every single one of her teeth. My mother was pretty then, hair the color of coal that twined loop-de-loops on each side of her cheekbones. Lips thin like a white woman's. Her body long, straight and upright like a cane stalk.

My mother and grandmother floated secrets around my grandfather's head. I made myself invisible, so I could know things that my grandfather didn't. He never knew about the nerve pills hidden in the bottom of my mother's brassiere drawer, or about the loud cursing sessions that my mother and my grandmother had. But I did.

I was fifteen and witnessing the end of one of these exchanges when I heard my father's name for the first time. My grandmother, dressed in an orange, fuzzy housecoat and slippers, stood between my mother and the TV. She shook a finger in my mother's face and said, "That is why, that is exactly why that good-for-nothing Leonard Eldridge left you high and dry with a wet ass and a big belly." I was bent over my homework at the kitchen table and pretended I hadn't heard a thing. I didn't dare look up, but a song was singing through my head. After my homework was done, after washing the supper dishes and climbing the stairs to my room, I wrote his name down before it danced away.

Leo-nard El-dridge, Leo-nard El-dridge. I looked in the mirror.

Girl, ain't you Leonard Eldridge's daughter?

Yes, I sure am.

Thought so. You the spitting image of him.

I pushed my nose toward the mirror for a closer look. Somewhere in my reflection, I could see my mother's nose and cheekbones, but I imagined my other features belonged to Leonard Eldridge. I examined myself trying to get a glimpse of my father. I took out a piece of notebook paper, wrote his name on it and tucked it underneath my pillow, hoping that a face I could recognize would turn up in my dreams.

I sat in Algebra, English and Social Studies writing his name on sheets of notebook paper, on my desk, and into the palm of my hand with red ink hearts all around it. As summer approached, everything about me that had always been wilted sprung up straight. It was the Leonard Eldridge in me working its way to the surface. Even my grandfather couldn't temper the wanting beneath my skin. Certain my family knew more about my father than they let on, I practiced sitting them all down in the living room. My mother in her chair, my grandmother in the rocker, and my grandfather stretched out along the couch. I stood in front of the mirror rehearsing, saw all their mouths gaped open and heard the hush come over the room. I wrote practice notes that, once they reached perfection, would be placed on the breakfast table beneath the sugar bowl to be found and read after I was safely in school.

One morning, the week before school was out, I stood at the sink brushing my teeth. In the mirror, even those parts that settled behind my teeth, under my tongue, and beyond the pink parts of my opened throat seemed to belong to my father. My grandfather had already left for the farm. My grandmother was somewhere already busy cleaning up white folks' houses. My mother was already up, showered and dressed, eagerly staring into the TV. I sat at the kitchen table eating my corn flakes and writing practice notes. I wadded them up, tore them into tiny pieces and deposited them into the wastebasket that hid beneath the kitchen sink alongside the ammonia and mousetraps. At the table, I tore a fresh piece of lined paper from my tablet and bore my number two pencil hard into the sheet. Each big block letter took up three lines and I

Daddy, Can I Tell You Something?

wrote: I KNOW LEONARD ELDRIDGE IS MY DADDY AND I WANT TO SPEND THE SUMMER WITH HIM. Short, direct, an open invitation for anyone who entered the kitchen.

Throughout the day, the paper and its bold scribbles haunted me. After school, I rode the bus home but didn't go inside the house. I caught a ride with Steve Wells, a white boy with a dark green Camaro. Two strikes, especially in this place where six Black families were scattered throughout the county like a half dozen raisins thrown against a hillside of snow. We were both invisible and seen too, too well.

"Where you headed?" I asked, leaning back into the seat and looking him dead in the eye.

"Wherever you want to go." He smiled. I turned my head toward the window, tried to quell the panic rising beneath my belt buckle.

"Up on the creek, to the farm," I said, trying to sound confident.

"Your folks up there today?"

"No." I saw the lines in his forehead raise up in a curious fashion, but I didn't let on like I noticed.

Steve's car eased onto the gravel road, stirring up dust. "I'm getting my car dirty for you," he said, looking over at me with a sly look. "You know there has to be a payback."

"No, I know no such thing." I said this while running my hands through my hair like a white girl. I knew he would like that.

When we reached a part of the farm that I was most familiar with, we got out of the car. I looked up at Steve, and he seemed taller than I remembered from English class. His shoulders seemed wider. He was cute, too, for a white boy. I was leaning back against the hood of the car. He stood over me cock-legged, his legs outside mine. His hair splayed out by the wind like yellow wings.

"Now what?" he said, drawing his face closer to mine.

"Now nothing," I said as I moved out of his grasp.

The trees had just begun to sprout bits of green, and the fields along the creek bank were still covered with vibrant pink, blue and white wild flowers. The air was fresh and clean, and I could see my grandfather's barn in the distance. I tried to picture my grandfather at home, gathering the women around him to discuss my Leonard Eldridge note, but I let that thought float out with the wind that rode in and out of Steve's hair. I slid down the bank, jumped the smaller part of the stream, ran across the gravel and ducked under the bridge before Steve caught up. When he slid down the embankment and came to a stop, I was already nestled into a nook, a spot just large enough for two people to fit into. He scooted in beside me, his hip jutting into mine. I hit him square in the shoulder and pushed him so hard he nearly fell in the creek. We both laughed.

"So what the hell?" Steve said, regaining his balance and moving in so close I felt uncomfortable again. "Why'd you want to come way out here?"

"Needed time to think." I left it at that.

Steve's daddy was always two-sheets-in-the-wind. His mother was scared of almost everything, especially his daddy. His sister, who was two years younger than me, was pregnant by some grease monkey over in Dunnville. Steve bought his car with his own money, working weekends with his Uncle Jessie. I grabbed his face at the cheeks and, just as our lips met, I noticed how white his face was, white as clouds, against my hands brown as caramel sauce. I had never kissed a boy before, but I opened my lips up to the size of a lemon, like the women on my mother's stories. Steve darted his tongue in and out of my mouth, and his hands wandered over me. I couldn't stop him. Didn't try. When I was sweetly exhausted from his touch, he buttoned my blouse, buckled my jeans and said, "Let me get you home." We stood up and hugged. I felt him hard down there on my leg.

I was silent in the car, my head still swimming, wishing this were a story that I could tell somebody. Back in town, Steve pulled his car onto 198, but I convinced him to let me out a long ways from the house. He pulled my face to him and livened my mouth with his tongue again.

"Gonna see you again?" he asked.

Outside the car, I looked around to see if anyone was looking, and I leaned into the car to kiss him one more time.

"Maybe," I said. I was still nervous. I felt his corn-silk hair brush against my fingers when I pulled myself away and then he was gone.

The night felt more like late fall than the beginning of summer, and I walked toward home with my arms crossed. A blue and white pick-up truck slowed beside me.

"I always wanted some nigger pussy," one of boys inside yelled, poking his red head out the window. It was John Grider from school.

"Whoo-hoo," another boy yelled from the truck.

"Let's get us some black tail," said a third voice whose face hid in the shadows.

The truck stopped, and I heard a door open. I ran, flying through yards and over fences. Far behind me, I heard laughing and the truck driving off in the opposite direction. I stopped to straighten my hair and pushed my shirt firmly back into my jeans when I got close to home.

Through the front bay window of our house, I saw my family gathered in the living room, each in their favorite evening positions, the white glare of the TV making them look like cartoons. Before I got a chance to turn the knob, I heard footsteps moving toward the door. My mother and my grandmother reacted at first in a way that I had not expected, smothering me with their "worried to death." I could see my grandfather on the couch through the arms and shoulders that fussed over me. He was rubbing his graying head which was bent low. In the kitchen, dinner was still laid out. Chicken and dumplings, roasted potatoes, carrots and peas. Cornbread. More fried apple pies. As I settled into the seat, my grandmother placed her hands on her hips.

"Girl, where in the hell have you been?"

"Just out thinking," I said, my eyes down into the plate. I

raised up long enough to drain the glass of grape Kool-Aid and accidentally brought it down too hard on the table.

"Just out thinking?" my mother said, making that hissing noise through her teeth. "I'm a give you something to think about."

My face was still stinging with the imprint of my mother's hand when my grandfather appeared at the kitchen doorway.

"The child wants to see her daddy. Send her and leave her be. Call up to Cincinnati and tell Leonard Eldridge his child's coming."

My grandfather's voice was strong and shattering and sent echoes, I was sure, of my father's name up and down the road. My mother's face contorted like she felt a pain somewhere, and my grandmother commenced to washing dishes and trying to scrub my father's name out of her house.

When I went to bed, they were whisper-cursing in a corner of the kitchen out of earshot like two teenage girls. But it stuck, Leonard Eldridge's name stuck like glue in the air filling up every empty space from the cellar to the attic.

That night, I fell asleep tasting my father's name on my tongue, but it was Steve Wells who I dreamed of all night long, his corn-silk hair flapping in the wind like a bird. I dreamed of me spent and quivering beneath his white hands.

Before I left for Cincinnati, Steve picked me up after school for five days straight. "Been thinking," is all I said when I got home late and somehow that was the only excuse I needed. Nobody questioned me anymore as if discovering my father warranted some reflection. As if we had all waited all my life for this. On that fifth day, as I lay gathering my breath, Steve unzipped his pants and pulled out his thing. It looked ugly in Steve's hand. Red. Veined. Throbbing. Not what I expected.

"You still a virgin ain't you?" he asked, rubbing his hand back and forth.

"Yes." I tried to say it with some confidence but it came out a low-pitched squeal. Steve turned his back to me. The wind caught

27

his hair, and he appeared to be about to take flight. His breath sped up and finally when it returned to calm, he turned back around, zipped his pants and held me close.

In bed the night before I left, I thought of my father. I tried to picture his wife, Tern, and the boys Mama called the stepbrothers. I wondered what Cincinnati was like. But mostly I thought about Steve Wells. It was a warm night, and, through my open window, I smelled the freshness of new, cut grass and listened to the crickets and the katydids. I snuggled down into the covers of my bed like it was the last night in the world that I would be nesting there.

At the Greyhound bus station in Stanford, my mother and my grandmother fumed over me, snapping the red windbreaker I was wearing right up to my chin.

"You call if them people don't treat you right," my grandmother said pressing two twenties into my hand. "You come home early if you want."

She kissed my cheek, leaving it wet. I felt it glistening in the morning sun, but I didn't wipe it off. My mother hugged me tight and said, "Have fun and you call as soon as you get there. Call collect if you have to."

She pushed me away from her but held me at the shoulders to get a final look. Then pulled me into her once more. "You look just like that damn man," she said, "your damned old daddy." This time she was smiling. My grandfather hugged me, too.

"Be good," was all he said, but I saw more hiding behind the thicket of his eyebrows.

"Bye. Love y'all," I said over my shoulder as I boarded the bus.

The bus driver, red and burly, tipped his hat toward me as he took my ticket. "Cincinnati?"

I nodded and scooted into an empty seat. The Greyhound bus smelled like piss. There were people everywhere. Crammed in like jigsaw puzzle pieces. A black-haired woman sat across from me with a little black-haired boy. The boy jumped and darted toward the window. Then the aisle. She made it her job for all the hours we were together to jerk and swat the child, who was a smaller version of her. She swatted his arms, his thighs. I guessed him to be four or five. There was a Black man behind me. He reminded me of Mr. Hershel from church. I wanted to talk to him because I saw a piece of home in him, but he ignored me and never looked my way. I saw a couple of brown-headed kids who looked as if they were on a honeymoon and a girl, much younger than me, traveling alone. Her copy of her ticket with her name, B-e-c-k-y, written in big red letters was attached to her blouse with a purple diaper pin. She smiled at me when she was not sleeping.

In Lexington, I changed buses. There were again no familiar faces among the many who climbed aboard the bus, but there were more Black people. There was a family. A girl about my age, a mother, a father, and a little girl who appeared to be in her two's. She was dressed in bright yellow and looked like a buttercup. The girl my age smiled. The mother nodded hello, but nobody spoke. Across the seat from me sat a couple in love. They kissed and giggled from Lexington to Cincinnati. The man, brown-skinned and dressed to the nines, kept one hand around the woman's shoulders like she was something too good to let go of. She was birdlike and light-skinned. There was something shy-looking about her. Her hair was swept up in a magnificent bun snaking along the back of her head. Her lips were painted pumpkin between the times that the man was not kissing away the color. Every time he kissed the rouge from her lips, she replaced it from the tube she pulled from the small pocketbook that rested in her lap like a kitten. I watched them and tried to picture my mother with my father like this, in love and running off.

Inside the bus station, there was a forest of Black men. Each time one came close or nodded or said "Hi," my heart beat a little faster. The tall, skinny, dark-skinned one with bell-bottom blue jeans. No. The short, light-skinned man with alligator boots. No. Seersucker pants. No. Hat tilted to the right. No. Freckles. No. Loud booming laugh. No. The fatherly looking man carrying a bouquet of flowers. No.

Finally, a dark brown man in blue work pants and a matching shirt approached me. The name "Leonard" beaming in white script across one shirt pocket. Norwood Plumbing on the other pocket. Not tall, not short. Not handsome, not ugly. An Afro. A pick stuck in the side. A small mustache. Nothing special. Nothing grand.

"Baby girl?" he said. He stretched out his arms, lean and bony like tree limbs, and scooped me up off the floor. He smelled of sweat and some spicy, sweet cologne. A smell I liked.

"Hi," I managed, not able to think of anything else to say.

He winked and smiled at me.

"Dead on your mama," he said, looking me up and down like he was searching for something familiar. I surveyed his face and saw only a hint of me there, beneath the eyes, I thought.

Leonard Eldridge's house was larger than I expected. It was red brick with a wraparound screened porch. Inside, everything was some shade of blue and most of it brand new. It smelled like I thought the ocean might. A feel-good smell. Spotless. There was thick shag carpet, a navy blue couch and matching chair. The walls were the color of the sky on a cloudless day. I had never seen anything like it. The three other members of my father's family entered the room, all from separate directions. Tern, my father's wife, hugged me so tight that I thought I would suffocate in her large breasts. She was dark with hips that spread out like two perfect cantaloupes on each side of her body. Dressed in tight jeans and a body suit, she looked like something about to pop open. I wondered what my father saw in her that he could not find in my mother's willowy frame.

"Look at you," she said. "Leonard Eldridge made over." And I giggled embarrassingly loud at yet another interpretation of who I was. The boys and my father looked like triplets. Leonard Jr. was fourteen, only one year younger than me, and Antwan was ten. They were dressed alike in green Izod shirts and matching plaid green and white shorts. Their dark faces were cleaned and lotioned. Right away I felt jealous that Junior carried my father's name. I had been his first-born child. I pondered the names Leona, Leontyne, Leonora, Leonard Etta, replacing each of them with my own. There was an uncomfortable quiet in the living room, all of us standing and looking at each other until my father said, "Boys, show your sister around." Antwan grabbed my suitcase with a ten-year old boy's determination.

"What you got in this thing?" he asked halfway up the steps. "Rocks?"

Junior just marched forward like a soldier carrying out his general's orders.

At the top of the steps, Antwan let my suitcase drop with a thud in the hallway. "Bathroom, my room, Antwan's."

Junior yelled out the rooms like the red burly Greyhound bus driver, only stone-faced. Antwan waved his hands like a circus ring master as he showed off his room.

"Ta-Da," he said.

"Dumb," Junior said, and pushed him to the floor. I laughed. "Mama and Daddy's room, kitchen, den."

The upstairs bathroom was done in zebra. Black and white tile. Rug. Shower curtain. Waste basket. Complete with ceramic zebras resting on the back of the toilet. Junior's room was sports. Basketball. Baseball. Football. A large orange basketball net was painted on his wall with a ball being released from large black hands into its open mouth. Antwan's room was cartoons. Fat Albert. Pink Panther. Bugs. Tweety. The room where my father and his wife slept was somewhere between American Black pride and Africa. Busts of Black women with large hoop earrings and large afros were on the night stand. African masks on the walls.

Daddy, Can I Tell You Something?

Leopard skin rugs, bedspread and curtains. Green vines snaking around the walls. Black panthers and lions that glowed under a blue/black light. The room they called mine looked like the sun. It was yellow and orange. Even the small bathroom attached was yellow and orange. There were tangerines, lemons and limes painted on the walls.

Tern served lasagna, salad and breadsticks for dinner. Not what I was used to, but I liked it.

"I want to spend some time with you tomorrow, Baby Girl," my father said. "It's been a long time."

I just nodded. Junior rolled his eyes, Antwan giggled, and Tern smiled so wide I thought her face would burst. I stared at my father between bites trying to find something more than ordinary that would make him the father I had imagined all these years, but I couldn't find anything.

Later that night in my room, I wrote to my family: I AM ENJOYING MY VACATION. MY DADDY LIVES IN A BIG HOUSE. THEY ARE VERY NICE PEOPLE. To Steve I wrote: I AM BORED AND WOULD MUCH RATHER BE HOME WITH YOU and signed it "Love, Leona," just for fun. I tossed and turned all night dreaming of my mother and father. They were the couple on the bus. Leonard Eldridge was unable to keep his hands off her. They were so much in love. Their lips pressed together every chance they got.

My father took me to the King's Island amusement park, the Cincinnati Zoo and to all his favorite restaurants. He held my hand like I was a little child and stared at me for minutes at a time. He asked me about school, boyfriends, interests and hobbies. I felt like I was being interviewed for a beauty pageant or a news show. I gave him generic answers and kept my disappointment in his ordinariness to myself.

"What happened?" I finally asked him during one of these outings. "What happened between you and Mama?" I asked again when he looked at me as though he had misunderstood.

"Baby Girl," he said after a long pause. Then he cleared his throat. "Sometimes......"

"What happened?" I repeated.

"I just didn't love her," he said, his head hanging down to his chest. "She was a nice girl. She told me she couldn't get pregnant."

Fifteen years and it had all boiled down to nothing. My father hadn't been madly in love with my mother at all. Leonard Eldridge looked me in the face, then looked away like he feared what he saw there.

"That don't mean I don't love you, Baby Girl," he said.

On the family outings, I felt like an outsider, a long lost cousin, maybe, but never like a daughter. There was always some family joke that I didn't get.

"Remember when we was at Disney World," Antwan said one night.

"No, I don't remember. I've never been to Disney World in my life," I said and went to the yellow and orange room and locked the door.

One Sunday when we were at a restaurant, me, Junior and Antwan were eating ice cream. We had all chosen chocolate. Our father must have seen a flash of a family portrait in that moment.

"Look at y'all," he said, "been eating chocolate ice cream since y'all was little things. Since before y'all could walk."

"You don't know a damn thing about me," I said and went outside and sat on the hood of my father's car until they were ready to leave. It was the first time I had cursed in front of adults.

I went home a week early. My father hugged me as we stood in the Greyhound station, but my arms wouldn't move to hug him back.

"Come back and see me, Baby Girl," he said, his voice cracking. I stepped on the bus refusing to satisfy him with a goodbye or a look back.

I returned home with a sharper tongue and rougher edges. I clanged the dishes in the sink and boldly walked in front of my mother's stories, daring a response. I was armed and ready, and she knew it.

I came home to find Steve riding a blonde girl around in his car. They could have been twins. Both tow-headed and skin so white. One evening, as I was walking home from Delk's Grocery, Steve pulled up beside me.

"I'm sorry," he said. "I miss you. Need a ride?" He knew I was mad about the girl in his car.

"Go to hell, you white, yellah-haired bastard," I screamed, and he drove off, his tires leaving a long black streak across the pavement. Every night, I cried myself to sleep and woke up more salty than the day before. I refused to talk to Leonard Eldridge when he called. I wanted my real father back. The one I had gotten used to not knowing.

On Thanksgiving break, Mr. Hershel's nephew, Stewart, came to visit. He was from Tennessee. He was just in town while his mother, Mr. Hershel's sister, had her gall bladder taken out. I summed him up in church. Dark-skin. Smooth as slate rock. Tall. Eyes like almonds. Hands big as dinner plates. My grandmother invited him and Mr. Hershel to our house for Sunday supper. After supper, outside on the porch, Stewart said, "What do y'all do way down here? I'd be bored shitless."

"I'll show you," I said, jingling the keys to my grandfather's LTD.

I took Stewart along the back roads to the farm up on the creek, dust blowing behind us like a tornado. Underneath the bridge, he kissed me softly, so soft I could barely feel his lips. His kiss was closed-lipped and sweet. I felt him shudder when I pried his lips apart with my tongue. I unzipped my jacket, unbuttoned my blouse, and let him touch me.

He stammered something, words I couldn't make out, his breath wild. When I took out his thing and pressed it against me, he hesitated.

"Don't worry. It's okay," I whispered.

Where You Been At, Daddy?

What I remember most is the quiet of Stewart's breath rising to a mechanical whine, his body drawn up tight as a fist, entering me like a weapon.

Hear Me Roar

(dedicated to Aisha who was brave enough to give me the seed for this story)

Angela Floyd

"You're sad," he said, inching close to me at the bar.

I was on my third glass of vodka, feeling fine. Vodka had been my drink since I was thirteen. I kept it in my closet in a box labeled "Keyetta's stuffed animals," mixed in with all the animals I got from my "uncles," my mother's pre-God boyfriends. I got the animals in exchange for keeping quiet about them being animals and trying to fuck me. If this guy was still near me after two more drinks, he'd hear all about it.

"Uncanny. I was thinking the same thing about you," I said. "You can't get anybody to dance with you, can you?"

I had brought this banter on myself by making eye contact with him. I couldn't take my eyes off of him. He was going after

36

all the ladies, big and small. He was getting completely and embarrassingly rejected, but he persisted. Maybe he was a player in his day, but not now. Now he was the old, skinny yokel in the tight olive green polyester suit with, yes, the matching shoes and a Duke home perm.

"You were thinking about me. Nice."

He really was sad. He turned away from me, distracted by an ass trying to escape from two-sizes-too-small black spandex pants and pretty much succeeding. As I looked at him then, he looked like he was once handsome, but he hadn't moved forward with everyone else. I wondered what had held him back. Probably prison. I went back to my drink.

"Seriously, what's wrong?" he asked.

He pushed an ashtray in front of me. I moved the tray back to my upper left-hand side where I always kept my ashtray.

"Okay, seriously, it's...it's just...." I pretended to cry until he pretended to be concerned, then I straightened up and told him what was wrong. "It's you. You're bothering me."

"Why?"

"Well, you're just so unimpressive. And your unimpressiveness is even more troubling because you're too old to be unimpressive."

The very idea of him was pissing me off. Men his age routinely pissed me off, especially when I could tell they were worthless husbands and fathers.

"You haven't seen me play pool."

"No, I haven't. You might want to hang out in clubs with pool tables so you can catch a chick because your current approach isn't working."

"What if I buy you a drink?"

"You don't see the one that I'm drinking?"

"I do. But you will finish that one at some point."

"Unless I nurse this one until I leave."

"But I can offer you a fresh one."

Daddy, Can I Tell You Something?

"*Touché.*"

"Latin. You must be in college. Nice."

"I must be in college because I said *touché?*" If I explained that the word was French he might have passed out from my genius.

"No. You're just sophisticated. You look real good. I've never seen skin that orange. It's exotic. You look real sophisticated with your hard drink and your cigarette and your hair all shiny and black and pulled back like that and the big words you use."

"I can see how that would make you think I was in college."

"I know you're not from around here. You're too beautiful."

I chose not to respond to that.

"So, if you're not in college. What do you do? Dancer? Model? Hairstylist?"

"I work at the library."

"See, I knew you were smart."

"I shelve books."

"But you read them, too, right?"

"Wow, you are looking right through me. Now, please go away. Don't you have a home? Kids?"

"No, I don't have anybody but me."

"You have kids, you just don't take care of them. Right or wrong?"

"Wrong. What's your name?"

"My name is Skyy, with two y's."

"Okay, Skyy, why are you here?"

"I am an alcoholic. I got stood up tonight. He didn't show and didn't even bother to call with an excuse. Now, tonight, I am getting drunk and looking for another man to mistreat me just to make it all a little worse." I routinely attracted the same men. Old pathetic men looking for young pathetic girls.

"Who would stand you up? Did he know how fine you are?"

"I guess not." I felt the well-up coming on. I turned away from him. I was ready to bawl, my signature drunk behavior.

I took another sip of vodka. I felt it burn as it cleared my throat and settled in my empty stomach. Vodka was truth. Pure and clear and satisfying. Consistent.

"Listen, I'll be right back, okay. I see somebody I know. I'll be right back."

"Don't come back," I said, but he was already gone.

I almost cried as I lost his back in the crowd.

I had waited for him all day. My doting father. I had finally tracked down the son of a bitch by stalking his mother whom I'd found by stalking a cousin. After I found my father's mother, I watched her house for two hours every day, but I didn't see any men coming or going. So, I approached her, questioned her, and got nothing. She said she didn't talk to him anymore and didn't know where he was. I asked for a picture since I'd never seen his face, but she said she didn't have one. I didn't believe her. I gave her my address and told her to tell him I was looking for him. She told me not to bother her anymore.

So next, of course, I started sending self-addressed stamped postcards to my father every three months via her address. On the postcard, I put three possible dates for us to get together, the third Saturday of each month, with a box for him to check. I had a clean process, but it didn't work.

Instead, after I'd stopped sending my postcards, I got a brief letter from him claiming to love me and miss me, apologizing for not being around, and requesting to see me. The letter was postmarked from Cleveland.

I had a full day planned for us. But as the morning he was supposed to come turned into the evening that he probably wasn't coming, I reviewed and modified our schedule repeatedly, while my mother stalked me. The letter was postmarked in Cleveland. He was here, and he'd show. My mother, however, wasn't going for it.

We only had a one-bedroom apartment. The bedroom was mine, but she had removed the door so she and Jesus could watch over me.

Daddy, Can I Tell You Something?

He was there even when she wasn't. She had a shrine to Jesus in the living room—candles, bibles, holy water, rosaries, framed posters of prayers, and a life-size cardboard cutout of the man himself. She had taken a perfectly good one-hour a week religious observation and turned it into an around-the-clock circus.

I liked Jesus, though. I even colored him brown. I thought she'd kill me for it, but she didn't. She came home, looked at him, looked back at me, and said, "I guess." I liked him brown. It made playing father and daughter more authentic for me.

Sometimes, when she wasn't home, I took Jesus to my room. He never tried anything. I even made a move on him once. I kissed him, and he still didn't try anything. He was my friend. My only friend. He didn't think I was weird. I shared CNN with him, the Desert Storm war coverage, all the violence and death and other bad news you could possibly want available all the time. I talked to him and asked him for his advice, while I counted the deaths announced on TV, matched the numbers with other sources, and looked to see if anyone I knew was among them, maybe my father. I'd asked Jesus if he knew where my father was and he'd say, "I've been looking, but even I can't find him. He's one slippery motha-fucka." Jesus was truth.

My mother, on the other hand, was a lie. The only people she could have a relationship with were her god, her Jesus, and her saints. Every other man she ever knew took turns fucking her to death in every way possible. They were a train that wouldn't stop running, that had no end, car after car crushing her beneath them until she was gone. Now, she was a universe of one and what she didn't want you to know, you'd never know. We didn't talk to each other that much. She worked, I went to school. I worked, she went to church. We paid our bills. In a few months when I finished high school, I'd move out.

"Keyetta, what do you think is going to happen?" she asked me. She took a break from shouting out scriptures. All day she'd been walking around me praying and chanting because she knew what I was doing. Jesus, blessed be the children, Jesus, praise God, save us, save her, Jesus, save her. I preferred her ranting over a conversation with her, but I knew one was coming.

"Keyetta, do you think he's going to do something for you? Do you think your father is going to walk through the door and make your life right?

"Maybe."

"You need to stop this. I'm telling you. Give it to God. Accept Jesus into your life as your father and let this go, or you are going to be your own downfall."

"I just want to know about him."

We'd had this conversation before. This fight had become predictably melodramatic. But at least I was aware of my bad girl-sad girl pathology. I think it's worse to be a wreck and not know you're a wreck.

"You already know about him. You want me to fix it up for you. Dress it up, so you have a good story."

"No."

"Yes, that is what you want, and I have nothing to say, praise God. I don't understand why this means so much to you. You're not an orphan. I'm here, and I've always been here."

"I didn't say you weren't here, Ma. But you didn't make me alone. I just want to know some things, anything, really. What's he like? Am I like him?"

"You're like you. I've told you before, the question is the answer. Figure out what you're really asking."

"What the hell are you talking about, Ma?" We were both insane, and I knew that, but I pressed on. "I'm asking you who my father is. Why isn't he here? Why isn't he in my life? He's got to have a reason."

"Keyetta, he's not here because he's not here. I'm here. I've given you food, shelter, education and Jesus, and that's all I've got."

Daddy, Can I Tell You Something?

"Why do you always do this? He's my father because you fucked him. You didn't fuck Jesus. You didn't fuck god. You fucked him. Now you want to keep secrets. Now you won't even say his name, tell me what he looks like."

She grabbed her chest where she must have thought her heart was, ran for the holy water and started sprinkling me, then herself.

"Holy water? That's your answer? That's your goddamn answer?"

She threw the whole bottle on me and ran for her bible. I went to my room where I waited until I felt as bad as I could stand to feel. And until my mother went to bed. I rolled my cigarettes in my hand and just smelled them because I couldn't smoke inside. Then I got out my vodka. I sat the bottle on my desk, my cup two inches from there, and my cigarette two inches from there. I sat and stared, and I waited until it was time to get fucked up, get dressed and go.

"I'm back."

I looked up from my drink. Everything was pretty, rinsed clean by my vodka. I stared hard at a man smiling at me. Death was in my chair. I thought of breaking my glass of vodka and slicing the pussyhound's neck.

"Why?"

"To see if you might want to dance or are you just here drinking your drink and looking beautiful tonight?" He was still at it.

"Drinking. That's all."

"So, can I arrange to take you out on a date and dance with you another time?"

"No."

"No?"

"No. I don't date. I've never been on a date, nor had any desire to go on a date."

"I don't believe that. How are you going to meet someone, get married, have a family?"

"I'm not having any kids. All I'd end up with is a girl who'd get fucked up by some man or a boy who'd fuck up some girl. The real issue is—why am I still talking to you?"

"You like me."

"No, that's definitely not it," I assured him as I put out my second cigarette and slipped off my stool. I nearly fell.

"You ok? Where are you going?"

"To the bathroom, if that's alright with you."

"Are you coming back?"

"No. And don't stand by the bathroom waiting for me to come out."

In the bathroom, I looked at myself between all the other bodies crowding the thin mirror on the wall next to the sink. Everybody was busy pushing and pulling and repositioning, hoping to change their lives by propping up their tits and getting their hair just right. The bathroom smelled like cigarette smoke, hair grease, perfume, liquor and pussy. Everybody in the room was just going to get fucked. Maybe not tonight, but certainly at some point soon. Maybe not by somebody in this club, but by somebody. Maybe a guy they would meet at church in the morning, or at work, or the grocery store. I smiled at them as I went into the orange stall because they all stopped to look at me.

"Shit." I tried to fasten the door, but the latch was broken. That, of course, made me cry. "Damn it," I wailed.

"What's the matter, baby?" someone said. "Oh, that door. Baby, that thing has been broke for months. The other one works, though. It's ok."

She shouldn't have known how long that door had been broken.

I backed out of the stall quickly, head down, and over to the next one hoping to avoid any conversation. It was locked. I ran out of the bathroom and headed for the exit.

"Hey. Hey. Wait."

I winced at the sound of his voice and kept walking.

Daddy, Can I Tell You Something?

"You leaving?"

"Yes."

"One dance. Please."

"Fine."

I walked to the dance floor with him. Everyone was slow dancing. All around me, big brown hands were gripping flesh. I closed my eyes and let him handle me.

I slid my pussy down on his dick slowly. I liked the feeling of that first penetration. It always had a newness to it. I could close my eyes and pretend that I was love. A cloud. A red daisy with flecks of pink and orange. An ocean. A snowflake. Peppermint ice cream. A little girl that nobody had fucked up yet. Anything but me. Anything but me in a motel on top of some guy whose name I didn't know.

Three strokes and he was out. I looked down at him. I always had to be on top because it wasn't intimate. No sweat dripping down on me. I didn't have to open my eyes to see blank eyes hovering above me. I held onto the condom and lifted myself off of him.

"You really are beautiful. I didn't think I was going to be lucky enough to be with you like this. I'll be looking around for you."

He got dressed in the bathroom, came out, and said goodbye to my back. I closed my eyes, smoked and rested for a while. Nothing about sex had changed since the first time. I don't know what I'm looking for, but I didn't find it then and still haven't.

I was 14. His name was John. I gave him some vodka my "Uncle Henry" had given me before my mother kicked him out so she could be with Jesus. I had some, too. I told John that he had to wear a condom. He was fumbling around and it was so dark that I couldn't see what he was doing. I was worried that I wouldn't know if he was wearing a condom because I didn't know what it would feel like with or without one. I'd only been grinded on by my "uncles."

"Is it on?" I asked him.

"Yeah. I said I would wear it."

"I didn't hear any paper tearing. Let me see if you have one on." I reached for the light switch beside my bed, but he grabbed my wrist.

"Damn, wait a minute. It takes a long time to get a condom on. Shit. You act like you ain't done it before."

"I am not playing, John. Do you have a condom on?"

"Why are you being such a fucking baby. We don't have to worry about a condom. I know you don't have anything."

"I'm not worried about me giving you something. I'm talking about you giving me something. And I don't want to get pregnant."

"Damn, Key. Hold on. You ain't really worth all this," he said as he pulled up his shorts and pants. He left holding his pants together with one hand. My bedroom window was open, and I could hear him asking his friends out on the street for a condom. I heard his friends tell him to use a plastic baggie. For some reason, he had some of those. He walked quickly back through the living room. I gasped as I heard him bump into Jesus.

"John, I heard that shit, you are not using a baggie with me."

"I got a condom, Key. Ok?"

He showed it to me. It really was a condom, so I was not off the hook. Not saying that I wanted to be. I just wasn't sure. Being with him felt just as shitty as being touched by my mother's men.

"Key, let me just feel you a little bit and then I'll put it on. I promise." He muttered the words as he moved around on top of me peppering my face and neck with quick dry kisses.

He was pushing his way inside me. His body locked into this awkward fixed rhythm.

"John, put the condom on."

His breathing got heavier and he made grunting sounds.

"Stop! Put the condom on! Put it on!"

I pushed up against his chest and tried to get my legs underneath

45

his to kick him off. It was too late. He collapsed on my chest.

"Sorry about that."

And that was it. My clothes were wrinkled and damp. What he left inside of me began to leak down my thigh. I just lay still in the bloody wetness for hours until I forced myself to get up to change my sheets and take a bath before my mother came home.

I felt sad, so I went out to sit with Jesus. I asked him if things would have been different if my father had been around. Would he have protected me? Jesus didn't say anything, so I thought that maybe everything that had gone wrong in my life was just meant to be. Maybe my father would have tried to fuck me, too.

On the way home from the motel, I couldn't stop thinking about my father. He had stolen my possibilities. One day, though, the bastard would come to see me. I would cook for him. A big meal of fried catfish, greens, macaroni and cheese, sweet potatoes and cornbread. Then I would lead him over to the sofa and make him look at every photo of me that my mother had ever taken, every award I had ever won, and every piece of junk I had ever made. I would show him all that he had missed. He would be reeling from the food and the speed with which I condensed almost two decades of history.

Then, I would shoot him. I'd shoot him right between his legs. Kill his sperm. Then, I'd shoot him in the kneecap so he couldn't run anymore, and he could feel the pain. Then, one shot to the head and two to the chest to ensure death. I imagined the bullets ripping through his skin and spinning through his body, splattering blood, organ fragments and undigested greens all over the walls.

Next, I would bury him in the park behind our building where he had never once played with me. He could never call me. He could never not call me. He could never stand me up again. I would know exactly where he was and what he was doing. No more imagining him having cheerful dinners with his beautiful wife and children. No more imagining him coming home to love me and staying. No more disappointment.

I smoked another cigarette outside our building just to tide me over. I slipped into our apartment quietly. I took off my club clothes and left them to soak in a sink full of cold water. After I showered and washed my hair, I put on my red and white striped pajamas, my favorites. I could have been any girl then. There was nothing that would tell anyone anything about me. My room was bare. No posters, toys, books, jewelry, perfume, nothing. My bed with plain white sheets and blanket. My desk empty except for one pen and a blank piece of paper.

I got up the next morning and brushed my teeth again to make sure the night before was gone. I stuck my head out the window to smoke a cigarette because I thought my mother was at church. But, I heard her voice in the living room. I put out my cigarette and popped a mint in my mouth.

"Ma?" I called as I headed for her voice.

"Keyetta." She met me at my door before I could even get out.

"What's wrong? Why are you crying?"

"Keyetta, your father is here."

I glared at her. She glared back.

"He's here." She said again. "He actually showed up. But you don't have to see him, praise God."

"Why wouldn't I want to see him?"

I looked at her wet face. For the first time, I looked into my mother's eyes, and she let me look. She was crying for me. I'd never seen him because he didn't care about me. That was the truth. Whatever had happened between my mother and father wasn't good. He was her pain, I was hers, and he didn't give a fuck about either one of us. That was the truth. I didn't know why he had showed up, but it wasn't because he loved me. I felt my little-girl self jump out of my body and run through my room. She never stopped until her body hit the concrete 10 stories down.

Daddy, Can I Tell You Something?

My mother reached for me. I shook my head and moved away. The one thing I knew is that I didn't want to be touched. No touching. Not her. Not him. Now that he was actually here, I had no desire to feel his arms around me. I just wanted to look at him. I would go and sit on the sofa across from him and look at him. See if I could see something to help me understand him. I didn't want to talk. Words are too tricky. You can't get to the bottom of anything with words.

"Ma, I'm okay." I smoothed back my hair, took a deep breath and went in.

"Oh god," I mumbled, stuck in my place in the room.

He had on the same suit from the night before.

"Oh shit. Oh god. No. No. No." He was backing away from me knocking down anything that was in his path.

"What?" said Ma, confused.

"I didn't know. Oh my god. How could I know?" His hands were shaking. His mouth moving.

He had on the same suit from the night before.

"Know what?" Ma asked looking from him to me, me to him, him to me. "Keyetta, what? Martin, what's wrong?"

Martin. I stared at him, mouthing his name. Every time I had asked her his name, she said that it didn't matter, and now it didn't. I looked from him to Jesus, to my mother, to Jesus and back to him.

If he would have just shown his face once. And why didn't he know me? If she would have shown me a picture. I backed out of the room. I couldn't take my eyes off of him. What kind of man doesn't know his own child?

I emptied out my stuffed animals and climbed into the box with a bottle of vodka. I could feel in there how sometimes there could not be enough room for the truth. I heard the door slam, and I heard the scream of his tires. He didn't tell her what happened.

She was calling me, but I didn't answer. I drank. Then I reached out my hand and broke the empty bottle of vodka on the closet wall. I brought the sharp glass to my arm and started cutting, but my mother stopped me before I could finish. She took the glass out of my hand, threw it, took off her sweater and wrapped it around my cut.

My mother emptied out the box next to mine and got in. She grabbed a bottle of vodka and started drinking.

"So, that's your father," she whispered. "But I don't understand what's going on. You want to talk?

"No."

"Well, do you want me to tell you some things?" She kept whispering.

"No."

I didn't want to say anything. I didn't want to know anything. Fuck her. I had my own past now. And I could only live if I made it a lie, a story I'd read, or a nightmare. It couldn't be my truth. He couldn't be my truth.

She unwrapped my arm and poured the vodka on the cut. I screamed.

"Go ahead and scream," she whispered.

The Reunion

Yetunde Lee

Twisting her tiny white-gloved hands in the sea-green foam of her crinoline, Ruby waited. The metal spokes of the creaking bench burned red welts beneath her narrow thighs. He was forty-five minutes late. A newspaper man sat down beside her with a big sigh and began chain-smoking Lucky Strikes. The hot smoke from his cigarette billowed angrily in her face. The sun seemed invincible as it arched against the eggshell blue sky. A pool of sweat began to gather beneath her breasts; in her rush, she had forgotten her talcum powder.

She remembered the last time, dressed in yellow sitting in the rain. But she hadn't learned that time, and here she was again. Each time he didn't show, he called at least three days afterwards. Her mother, Eunice, said that was so he could cheer them up and fatten their slender hopes of seeing him again. Now, she was the only one left with the fat greasy airy hopes. Little girl blue. He used to call her that way back when they danced beneath the naked bulb in the kitchen. She remembered her tiny pink toes riding his big black socks as they slid across the yellow striped linoleum. His big mouth open in a loud hungry laugh as she struggled to stay atop his big feet, hooking and jiving to the beat.

Ruby took off the white gloves. Eunice had told her it was useless to wear the lovely gloves to see such a "no count bastard." Eunice hated him. She hated him for leaving, but even more since that first time he stood them up. Her wrath would snake out smacking red hot against the pasty white walls of their apartment. His infrequent calls, once every three to five months, and always at midnight, "cause it was nine in LA" the city "where things are happen'in, man," would spark screaming rages for days. The first time he had not shown up, Eunice had hand sewn a pink and yellow dress edged in white ribbon for Ruby. She spent three weeks on the dress, sewing by the light of a slight piece of moon. That Sunday morning when he was supposed to arrive, Ruby and Eunice held hands at the crossroads of town, heads up, backs straight, facing the early morning breeze. Four hours later, the white ribbons of Ruby's dress were bathed in the road's red dust.

Ruby wrote him. Her letters came back cold, travel weary, with a "Return to Sender" stamp on the envelopes. Once when a letter came back, Eunice began quiet murmurings into the burning flames of red candles. The candle burning was supposed to send him all sorts of evil spirits, according to Ma Lucia, the conjure woman. She had Ruby's umbilical cord burned, knotted and buried beneath a great wide Spanish oak tree to help matters.

One year, the birthday gift Ruby had painfully worked to purchase came back unmarked and unopened. Eunice cursed every hair on his head. That fall evening, as windy gusts spun against the indigo heaven, Ruby's own pain rushed up and swelled in her throat. She blamed Eunice and her evil intentions. Racing about, tripping on the hem of her sweetheart nightgown, Ruby turned over the candles and almost burned down the place.

Daddy, Can I Tell You Something?

Now she sat demure and patient. The old man next to her slowly lifted a butter-heavy biscuit from a sticky bag. Ruby stood, her high arching breasts pressed against the airy material of her dress. Lifting her white Sunday hat, she swept a drop of sweat off her forehead with the white lace baptism gloves Aunt Cellie had bought just this morning.

Nervous, she checked the square-faced clock. The roman numerals read twelve o'clock. One hour had passed. When Ruby was on her way out the door this morning, Eunice told her to leave after ten minutes if he hadn't showed up. But she continued to wait. The seconds clacked away, stretching out her waiting like a rubber band. Tapping the white sandals shined with chicken flit two nights ago, she thought of his call.

She was standing in the kitchen, in a pool of yellow sunshine, snapping green beans. Watching Eunice hanging fresh clean clothes, she lost herself in the bright blue skies painted with wispy flour-white clouds. The telephone broke her afternoon reverie.

"You goin' pick it up, Rube?" Eunice yelled through the wide open window.

Ruby lifted the receiver with a snapped bean stuck to her palm. "Hello?"

"Ruby? Rube? That you?" The voice spilled across the line, sweeping her breath away. She stared out the window, completely still.

"Oh Ruby I'm so glad I got you. I know its been a while and everything, but I thought I'd call anyway." His soft mellow voice rushed ahead. "How are you? How are things?" He paused. "Hello?"

"Ruby, it's me."

Her voice was still locked away in the dry heat of her mouth.

"Uh, uh, I can't believe this," she finally answered.

"Yeah, I know it's been awhile, baby, jest give me a minute."

"Is it really you?" she whispered, coughing through the words that crowded her mouth.

52

"Yeah, Rube, it's been too long, and I know last time I missed you, but I got some special stuff from New Yark jest for you."

Ruby began to inhale slowly. Cool white air rushed into her lungs and she smiled.

"I was wondering if we could get together, 'cause I'm close by, jest ten miles away."

Ruby watched as a white sheet dotted with blue flowers billowed in Eunice's arms.

"Can we maybe get together next week, next Friday morning?"

She was still silent.

"Hello? Rube?"

"Okay," she said, smiling into Eunice's eyes. "It's on."

"Okay? Did you say okay? You said okay! Oh, Ruby you're too much, giving me another chance like this!"

Ruby watched Eunice's face. Her mother had stopped folding and the clothes hung limp in her arms.

"Okay, baby, so I'll see you then?" he asked.

"Yes, definitely."

"All right, Rube, now you know what, Luv?" he asked sweetly.

"What?" she crooned.

"I love-"

Suddenly, Eunice was in the tiny kitchen, large black outstretched fingers snatching the phone from Ruby's hand.

"You fucking low-life bastard," she growled into the receiver. "You promising again," she screamed and slammed the phone down. Her narrow almond-shaped eyes blazed as she bore down on Ruby.

"I will not be involved, Ruby. I will not watch you be let down again. You can get yourself to this meeting place. Where is it this time that he wants to humiliate you? The bus station? The crossroads? Downtown?"

Deflecting her mother's anger, Ruby calmly returned to snapping the beans. In a plain solid voice she said, "The train station. And you don't have to go this time. I understand."

Daddy, Can I Tell You Something?

And with quiet sweetness, a cloud of pink cotton candy surrounding her, she washed the beans and began to hum a tune under her breath.

A white woman wearing a thin rose-colored dress and carrying a golden-haired baby boy marched onto the platform. Bits of olive in the baby's gray eyes shone in the sunlight. The woman smiled as Ruby made room for them on the bench. Looking at his innocent, hopeful eyes reminded her of her own hopes pinned on this moment.

Getting out her best crinoline dress, Ruby let out the hem, pressed the pleats, lovingly sprinkled it with lavender water and finally hung it up in her room. She borrowed Eunice's shoes and shined them diligently while she planned on leaping into his arms and kissing his big black face. In the morning, as she hot-combed her hair, she gazed out the window dreaming of sipping mint tea, while the two of them swung lazily in Eunice's homemade hammock out in the yard. She dreamt of telling him of all that he missed as they rocked in the peach-scarred light of dusk. Wrapped up in his thick muscled arms, she would gaze into his smiling eyes. Eyes that would only see the beauty and purity of her soul. All of the past hurts would vanish in one instant. She would tell him how devoted she had been, waiting patiently knowing he would come back just like he promised. Together they would escape Savannah's broiling heat and endless rains, off to California they would fly.

All the dreaming tired her. Hoping a train would appear, she began to negotiate with God. Ruby's deals with God had been a lifelong practice she had started when she was five. Eunice had been struck down with an awful sickness that made her rant and rave like a crazed woman through the nights and sleep coma-like through the day. Ma Lucia was called in, and Ruby could remember the forlorn look in Ma Lucia's eyes as she began her incantations. For thirteen nights, Ma Lucia moaned and burned incense while Ruby, on her tiny cot, made silent deals with God.

"If you make my Mommy better, I promise not to steal sweets from Jude's lunch."

"If you make Mommy better, I promise to help Debbie wash the clothes every Saturday."

As golden rays blasted her copper skin, she shut her eyes and made another deal with God.

"Just bring him this time and I'll forgive all the stuff from the past."

"If you just bring him this one time, you can take him away and never bring him back, but please, oh please, bring him this once."

Gripping her hands together, she opened her eyes, waited a beat, then slowly tuned her ears to the sound of metallic rumbling.

"Sounds like that may be it, darl'in," the white woman cooed to the baby. Unfolding her long lean body, Ruby stood slowly and peered down the tracks. The huge black train screamed, almost breaking the afternoon's palpable heat. As the train screeched to a halt, Ruby froze watching the faces, bodies, smiles, open arms, and loping gaits as the passengers disembarked. People began to storm the tiny station. Faces. Faces. Faces. And more faces. The newspaperman immediately began to hawk his papers.

Her palms sweating, she peered through the crowd, searching. She gripped her purse, trying to find his face, an aged face now, that stood lonely in an old frame on her dresser. Sharp jawbones. Keen nose. An elf-like upturned mouth. Beautiful eyes. High molded cheekbones. Beautiful, simply too beautiful. Eunice had often said that he was too beautiful to be a man, that God usually reserves that kind of good looks for women.

Ruby stood silently, staring, as tides of people tossed and rolled about her. It seemed as if the sun had cooled its rays for just this moment. Glancing away for just a second, she looked at the clock. One o'clock. She recorded the time then slowly turned back to the train and looked into his face. There he was, walking slowly toward her. He didn't see her. Of course, he didn't know it was she. But there he was all the same. A bolt of joy shot through her as she began to run. Her long legs stretched in desperate but graceful strides. She ran faster, thinking of his arms, the ones she could see now, wrapped tight around her slim body. Anticipating the feel of his warm brown skin, she tore off the lovely white gloves and ran into his arms.

"Daddy!" she cried.

Sepia brown eyes flashed on hers, uncomprehending. Exultation raced through her veins, as she felt warm in his arms.

"Daddy!" Wrapping her thin arms around him, she pulled her head back to look at his face. To see his joy. Instead, her eyes fell on a horrific sight: Eunice racing toward them, murder in her eyes. With her arm arched high, she ran toward them.

"Aiehhh!" Eunice wailed swinging her arm down.

"Noooo!" Ruby cried, twisting her father about to shield him. Her thin body blocking his as they fell to the cool concrete of the station platform. The great clock slowed. Sunlight shrank against the cold slate-gray sky as Eunice's kitchen knife plunged into Ruby's slender back. Silence fell over the crowded station.

Bent doubled over the work of her hands, Eunice realized what she'd done. Her howls shook the station's frame.

"Oh no! Ruby, my baby, my baby, Ruby!"

****

Flattened against the cool concrete, the man searched the station for his wife from beneath Ruby's body. Bewildered by these two wild screaming women, he felt the strange girl's last breaths rattle away.

New Born

Walidah Imarisha

Dear James,

I started this letter an hour and a half ago and only got as far as "Dear." It seemed odd to address it "Dear Father." "Mr." is plain stupid and connotes a power relationship that makes me uncomfortable. So, although it seems presumptuous of me to call you by your first name, James it is.

You probably didn't even recognize the name on the envelope. Almost three years ago, I legally changed my name to Walidah Imarisha. I spent most of my life trying to find a name that fit. The one you gave me never felt right. My new name means "new born strength." It is pronounced "Wal-ee-duh Ee-mar-eesha."

Recently, I was watching a sappy movie about a Black woman's search for roots and ties to the past, about her efforts to ground herself after being blown around by any passing wind. By the end of the movie, I was bawling.

Even before then, I'd been thinking so much about who I am and where I come from. But I can only get so far because I hardly know anything about you. My mother told me that I got my stubbornness from you. And my long fingers. She looks at them and says they remind her of you playing the guitar, says she can even hear you plucking out your favorite song, "Sitting on the Dock of the Bay," my favorite song, too. Must be some form of genetic encoding, because I loved that song the first time I heard it. After she told me you loved it too, I imagined you sitting at the edge of a pier somewhere, staring out into a vast sea. It made me so immensely sad, I couldn't bear to listen to it anymore.

This was all I learned about you, and I decided not to ask for more. I preferred to live my life without knowing when I inadvertently stepped into the shadow of my distant father. It hurt too much.

As I get older, though, I realize I have no idea what you think about anything. I am a history major, and my focus is on the Black Liberation era of the 1960s and 1970s. You lived through it, and I wonder what it was like for you. What did you think of the Black Panthers? You lived in the South then, and I can't even imagine what that was like for a young Black man at the time. I hear other people's stories, but never yours. What was it like to be dating my mother, a white woman, in 1979? What was it like to have a mixed child then? What did you think of me? Was I beautiful to you? Were you proud? Did you take me around to family events? Did you cradle me in one arm while you casually nursed a beer, the hot air vibrant around us? Did the barbecue sizzle through exclamations of "Oh, James, she's adorable! Look at her! She's like a little doll!" Did you grin with fatherly pride? Was it like that or is that just me creating scenes from dust? Because the only real memories I have of you are hazy: you sitting on a worn couch in a friend's Mississippi house. I can't even remember what you said, if you hugged me, if you lifted me up, or if you told me you loved me.

I met a man on the bus a couple of years ago. He asked me why I sounded so white when I spoke. At the time, I had not formulated my identity so clearly. I was just tired and irritated by the question, and yet I felt compelled to answer it. So I told him I was mixed. He asked who raised me, I told him my mother. He asked where my father was. I told him I didn't know. He asked if I ever spoke to my father, and I said not in more than ten years. Then, he got a sad look in his eyes, and he said that he could hear the anger in my voice, that I could be his daughter because she hadn't seen him in so long either. He said that he loved her with all his heart and thought about her every day, and I wondered if you felt the same about me.

I have been angry at you, but it was more of a concept and a principle than an actual feeling. Since I've never had a father fulltime, I can't say that I miss it. That doesn't mean, though, that I don't know that I'm missing a part of me.

You were not strong enough to stand by me and shield me. You gave what you could, I guess. But if you had stayed, perhaps you would have been able to reach deep inside, to pull up something to give, something to share. Mom saw something in you. She loved you still after so many years and so much abuse from you. She didn't tell me how you hurt her until very recently, when I finally asked her. I will ask her more about you because, perhaps, until I walk down that road of memory with my mother, clutching her hand, sharing in her laughter and her screams, I won't be able to know you. Maybe if I learn about you I can understand you, maybe even love you. For now, though, that love can only be with open eyes and a guarded heart.

In strength and struggle,
Walidah

A Letter to My Father on My Forty-Sixth Birthday

Opal Palmer Adisa

If I've forgiven you like I've said, then I should be able to write "Dear Daddy" without hesitation, yet I cannot. So how should I address you? What feels comfortable? I remember my letter to you fifteen years or so ago. I addressed you by your first name, Orlando. You did not respond to me. Instead, you told my sister that I was being impertinent. I was angry, but mostly hurt by your dismissal. I felt I was being punished for daring to ask for an explanation, for demanding accountability from you.

I went about my life trying to erase you from my memory.

We didn't communicate for years, though you wrote to my children and included a footnote asking them to say hello to me. What was that all about? Pride? Parental authority? The need to have the upper hand?

Why can't you say "I am sorry. I messed up." I loved you even when you didn't hear from me for those ten odd years. I was loving you and kept you in my heart. Maybe there is some unwritten rule that parents should not apologize to their children, should not admit to being wrong. I do not subscribe to those rules. I mess up more often than I would like and have to say to my children, "I am sorry, I was wrong. I messed up, but I love you."

I don't expect an apology from you anymore, Mr. Palmer, but I do deserve one. You owe it to yourself, to me, to our ancestors, to clean your heart before you die, to make peace with your adult children. And that is what I am, an adult, not the little girl who called you Daddy. I am my own woman. I have the right to my feelings, regardless of whether you think I am justified in those feelings. If we are to have a relationship, it has to be as one adult to another trying to find our way back to each other to connect in this present moment.

I know the past cannot be re-written, and I wish my memory was less remarkable. I also know that, like you, my memory is fixed on my own hurts, and I am unable to see the bigger picture. I know how much you must regret not witnessing my transformation into a young lady. For the past three months, I have been away from my children working. I feel as if I have missed out on large chunks of their lives, and I don't want to miss out any more. So, I suspect I know the depth of your longing because my memory of you from my girlhood is vibrant. When I see you inside my head, it is mostly all good.

My first memory of you was planted by my mother. She told this story often when I was growing up. She said that when I was two years old, I had climbed to the peak of a guava tree but was unable to come down. You climbed as far as the branches would withstand your weight, then told me to jump. I jumped and you caught me.

I don't remember that. Memories of you of which I take ownership are these:

Daddy, Can I Tell You Something?

You are laughing and drinking and joking with friends on the veranda. You are walking around the yard in only shorts, gardening and washing the car. When I was no older than four years old, you put me on your lap and allowed me to steer your car, and I almost steered it into a canal.

You wrecked your car while traveling to Kingston. The whisper is that you were drunk. I remember when you came home from the hospital and had to be fed with a straw because you had injured your jaws as well as broken your leg. It was a miracle that you had survived. As I stood back watching my mother spoon-feed you, I cried for all the pain you were suffering.

I remember the day my mother, sister and I piled in the truck with all our belongings. You stood on the veranda and watched us leave, but you did not wave goodbye to us. A few months later, you came to get us, but the maid called my mother at work. My mother came home during the middle of the day with a policeman who told you that you couldn't take us; we had to stay with our mother. My sister wanted to go with you, but she also wanted to stay with our mother. I said that I wasn't going with you.

I remember you came to either my sister's birthday party or mine; I don't remember whose, but it was not long after my mother left you. Everyone left, but you refused to go. My mother begged you to leave. Finally, she locked the door and left you sitting on the veranda in the dark. I worried that you had to sleep there alone.

I remember spending part of the summers with you. Every Sunday, you took us to Gun Boat Beach before the beach was officially open. We crept under the wire. The water was usually a little chilly, but you took my sister and me, one at a time, on your back and swam way out of sight. While I waited on the shore for your return, I wondered if you would be able to swim the distance. You seemed so far.

I remember staying with you in the tiny apartment you shared with that woman you later married and whose child, I later learned, was my sister. We always had dinner when you came home from work. We had to sit quietly around the table, not talk while we ate, use our knife and fork at all times and no elbows on the table. I remember Pretty Parrot, our pet, with its emerald green feathers. You taught him to speak. Each day, you cleaned his cage and gave him a small red pepper. Sometimes you would place Pretty Parrot on my shoulder, or you showed me how to hold out my arm for him to stand on it. I remember those Sunday drives, sitting in the back of your car in our Sunday dresses with matching ribbons in our hair.

I was eight years old when your father died. We all stayed at his house, even my mother. You were busy taking care of all the details. The day of his funeral, you and the other male relatives dressed him for burial. You came and got my sister and me from the large yard where we were playing with cousins we'd just met. You led us into the cold room with your father's body. You lifted and passed first me, then my sister, over grandpa's body for protection. Then you helped me help you put on his socks. I remember it had been raining on and off the entire time we were there. I would often go into the room where Grandpa lay covered with ice to peek at him and to see if he would get up. But he never did, not even when I took a handful of ice-mint from the sweetie jar on the counter. People said I was brave, not being afraid of the dead.

A few years later your sister, Aunt Lyn, died. She never made it home from the airport, returning from the United States. The talk was that she had worked herself to death there. I remember your closed tight face at her funeral.

Finally, I remember a party at your mother's house. You arrived late. Though mother looked beautiful, you didn't speak to her because you had your wife. I remember people whispering about you at the party.

My memory fades after that. I was only ten or maybe eleven. No pictures of you again until I am twenty and graduating from college. By then, we had moved with our mother to New York where we heard you had been. We never saw or heard from you the five years we were there, until we received a letter from you one day. You started the letter with "Dear Daughters" and wrote as if we hadn't been out of contact with each other for all those years. Where had you been? Why had you suddenly contacted us? Your mother, our grandmother, always knew where we were, and you always knew where she was, so why didn't you write or send birthday cards?

Daddy, Can I Tell You Something?

I have rehashed the past tirelessly, but my analyzing and reanalyzing was pointless because the past cannot be changed. All we have is the present, this moment to live our lives with love and forgiveness and understanding. I want to feel comfortable with you. I want to make peace, truly. But I want an explanation, some way of bridging the past. I want my children to know you. I want to hear them call you Grandpa. I want them to sit on your lap and have you tell them stories. I want to share with them the fond stories I have of you.

I want to be able to call you by a name, but it cannot be Daddy. We missed that moment. If you don't want me to call you Orlando, I will call you Mr. Palmer. If you don't want me to call you that, then what? I cannot call you Daddy. I am not your little girl. I am a woman of forty-six with three children of my own, and I have weathered the storm without you.

This year, I received a birthday card from you and it comes as such a pleasant surprise. What does it mean, I wonder? Are you willing to see me as the woman I have become? Are you willing to treat me as an adult and respect my reservations as much as you are demanding that I respect yours? Do you want to call a truce and allow us to enjoy the rest of this time we both have in this place? I don't know.

In my imagination, you and I grew up together. You watched me mature, and I watched you age. I would tell you about the men I fancy, and you would give me advice about what to do. Mostly, you would encourage me to be myself, to follow my dreams relentlessly and to always live with integrity and honesty. And if, like now, we live in separate states, we would call each other weekly. We would write to each other regularly, and you would tell me about your life as a boy and then a young man. We would visit yearly, and my children would run around and mess up your neat home or fumble through your old mildewed photo albums. You and I would talk over a cup of tea or while strolling through your garden. Our arms would be hooked, and we would talk and laugh and lean on each other, happy that we are father and daughter. Then when I returned to my own home, I would sit at my desk and write you this letter:

Dear Daddy:

I am so grateful that you are in my life, and that you are my father. Words cannot give flavor to the joy I felt seeing you with your grandchildren, my children, and how much my youngest is like you. I don't think I knew that before our recent visit. I so enjoyed the candid talks we had. I am so thankful that you accept me for who I am, and that you listened to me and really heard me. I am pleased that you are able and willing to share so much of your life as a gift with me. We are all the wealthier for sharing so abundantly with each other. I have taken your advice about the tomatoes, and mine are already looking better. Thanks, too, for the gentle way you told me to slow down and not try to take on the world all at once. I want you to know that I really heard your love and worry for me, and I am going to make some major changes because I don't want to take years off your life from worrying about me.

Your grandchildren really enjoyed the time they spent with you. They especially loved the stories you told them about your father, and how he came to be the owner of a store. I hadn't heard that story before.

Daddy, I wish you and I could travel to Jamaica, visit your father's land and go to his grave and thank him for helping to bring you into the world. Then you could show me the place where you grew up and point out the trees you climbed and the rivers you swam in, and the people you knew and where they lived. I wish all of us could take a trip back there and stop at Gun Boat Beach and take a swim and let the soothing salt water refresh us. We could visit your mother's and sister's graves and mourn and celebrate their lives. Maybe we could even get another parrot like the one we had and call him Pretty Parrot 2. Daddy, I am glad you are proud of me, and I want you to know how important it was to have you say that to my face and to kiss my cheeks and hold my hands, and call me your little grownup girl.

Daddy, Can I Tell You Something?

I love you Daddy. I love you, and daily I thank the divine creator that you joined with my mother to have me.

All my love, Daddy. I'll talk with you soon.

Walk Good,
Your darling daughter, Opal

Dear Sir

Tanya King

I'm twenty-nine years old now, Sir. I have been searching for you all these years. Without ever having met you or even knowing your name, I searched for you.

When I was a little girl, I searched for you in the night hoping you would come into my room to protect me from the scary shadows that crept outside my window and made shapes in the darkness on my bedroom walls. Instead, I held my Teddy Bear, shut my eyes tight and prayed that a prince would come to save me.

I searched for your big hands to hold my tiny fingers as I walked to school in the mornings. Instead, I held onto little Kevin who lived up the street. His hands were as small as mine. He wasn't big enough to protect me from the world, but he cared, and he arrived on time every day, before and after school.

I searched for your strong and guiding hands on the back of my bike as I learned how to ride. Instead, I had to steady myself. You

67

weren't there to teach me and keep me from falling. You weren't there to assure me that I could do it.

I searched for your words of wisdom as I wondered if I should give my virginity to my high school sweetheart. Instead, I had to make the decision by myself. I wasn't sure what to do, so I gave it to him. He told me that he loved me. He was the first man to ever tell me that.

For years, I searched for you in the arms of men who promised to protect me and love me endlessly, but didn't. I searched for you in men who cradled me in their arms, whispered in my ears reassuring me that my deep black skin, kinky hair, broad nose and thick hips were royally beautiful. I was desperate for their affection and adoration. I accepted their gifts, let them call me baby and even called them Daddy if they made me feel special. But it was never enough.

I searched for your arm, interlocked with mine as I walked down the aisle on my wedding day. Instead, I gave myself away, Sir. Instead, I omitted the father-daughter dance from the wedding program.

I searched for your concerned eyes peering inside the door to my hospital room to check on me as I gave birth to my first and only child, a little girl. I wanted to rest my head on your shoulder when she died shortly after her birth. But I was alone, Sir. Her father was absent that special day, too. And I thanked God for allowing her to leave this life so soon, sparing her from the sorrow of searching.

It was your job as father to teach me what to expect from men, what to ask for, how to ask for it. It was your job to teach me how to love and receive love. Instead I learned to expect nothing, to be happy about having a man present, even if he wasn't there spiritually and emotionally. I don't know how to have a healthy relationship with a man because you were not there to show me by loving my mother and me. You should have been there, Sir. You should have done your job.

I am sure that one day the realization of all that you have missed will hurt you as much as it has hurt me, and I will pray for you.

May God continue to keep you, Sir, wherever you are.

Loving you always,
Your Daughter,
Journey

Wish Letter

Shari Taylor

Dear Dad:

I wish I could call you Daddy again. I wish I could sit on your lap and lean back in your arms safe again. I wish we were on a car trip, the whole family, in your old station wagon. I wish it was Christmas morning, and we were racing downstairs to a land of toys. I wish it was Wednesday night, and you were home in the front room watching "Lost In Space."

I wish you and Mom hadn't split up. I wish you had cared enough to stay in touch more than once every three or four years. I wish I didn't know what foodstamps look like. I wish I hadn't watched Mom pick coal out of ashes to keep us warm. I wish I hadn't seen her wear the same shoes for five years with the same coat and the same tired stoop in her shoulders. I wish I hadn't watched her grow old too early. I wish she hadn't died.

Where You Been At, Daddy?

I wish you had been there for birthdays and picnics and school plays and dodge ball and bedtimes. I wish you knew who gave me my first kiss and who was the first to break my heart. I wish you had taught me how to drive and helped me pick a college. I wish you'd seen me graduate. I wish you'd been there to protect me from men who only wanted to hurt me. I wish you had advised me on buying my house. I wish you had held my hand when I had surgery because of cancer.

I wish I didn't only see you at funerals. I wish you knew my name from my sisters' without having to think about it. I wish you knew my favorite color, or what makes me laugh. I wish it hadn't taken you thirty years to want to know me. I wish I had trust in you. I wish it wasn't too late.

I wish I could call you Daddy again.

Shari

Daddy Needy

Sharon Dawkins

i know i will never understand
how hard it is for you to be a man
but daddy
what happened
what went wrong
that made you leave your little girl
all alone
mama didn't like me
i reminded her of you
you just like yo fava
you just like yo fava
that's what she would say
she wouldn't give me no time
she always turned away
i withdrew
withdrew
it was all i could do
rejection from her
rejection from you
now i went and done the one thing
i swore i'd never do
daddy
i went and married a man
just
like
you

my daddy brought me bunnies

Virginia Merritt (based on a story told to her in her work as a social worker)

i have these thoughts. i have these thoughts alla time 'bout goin' up to the roofnjumpin off. i go up there an the po-lice haveta come or the fire trucks, but they can't stop me. I jump offa the roof an go to where my granddaddy is. he was the one took care a me when my mom drank an socialservices come. now i wanna be with him where he is.

my father's in jail. he killed a cop. my father's in jail an i don't wanna be there. i was in jail one time for assaulting an i don't wanna be there again.

i hate my father. last time I saw him tho he was real nice. he brought my mom a ring. he comes in. i say who's that man? my mom say he's your daddy. i say that ain't my daddy. i ain't seed my daddy since i was real little. but she say no, that's yo daddy, go up an say hi to yo daddy. so i goes up to him an hugs him an says i love you daddy an he says i love you punkin an then he says i got somethin for you. he's all smilin. he's got his hands behind his back. an i go what what what what you bring me? an then he brings out

Daddy, Can I Tell You Something?

somethin with a blanket thing over it. i go what is it what is it? an he picks up the blanket thing an inside is—BUNNIES.

my daddy brought me bunnies. i named mine Tinky-Winky an my sister named hers LaLa. one of the bunnies they was all white an soft. one of them had a colla, an the colla had a box on it an my daddy picks up the bunny an hands it to my mom an says look an she says what's this n he says jes look an she takes the box off the colla an opens it up. it's a ring an she opens her mouf an looks at mydaddy an then she holds the box up against her heart like they do on tv an she says oh oh oh an then she says i can't take this an he says yes you can an she put it on her finger an hold her hand out an look at it an he come back for a few months an we were a family.

then one day he just leave for work an never come back. how he do dat? just leave for work an never come back.

my mom she never get married. she say she don't wanna get married. she wanna be free. that's what she say. i wanna be free too. i wanna jump off the roof. be like a bird flyin free through the air.

II. Daddy, Thank You

I Knew His Face

Jeanette Drake

I knew his face
when I was four and five and six
and skipped up unpaved sidewalks every afternoon
to meet him thirty minutes
after the shipyard's whistle blew.
His skinny arms reached down
to grab me from the dust.
I'd never heard of Robert E. Lee
or Fort Monroe. All that mattered
was I belonged
to this tall man.
When supper came
he was there
to peel hot skin from baked yams
or make lemonade better
than what the Queen of England deserved.

The More You Work Your Mind

Leila McCullough

It was a cool, almost-fall morning when the white man came to our house.

"Lee," he said, "I've gotta get that cotton out of the field. I need all your children working for the next couple of weeks."

Daddy said nothing for a while. Then he looked straight at the white man and said, "I'm not raising cotton pickers. My children hafta go to school."

The man said, "Well, then, I need this house for a family who's willing to work."

Daddy didn't say a word, but I knew what that meant. We were moving again. We moved so much we had it down to a science. Sometimes we wouldn't even unpack. Daddy would say, "Don't unpack cause we won't be here long." When he said that we knew it was true.

That was my life as a child. Packing, moving and going to

school. Daddy's children did very little work, unlike most of the children that we knew. Daddy would say, "I work like a dog so my children don't haf to."

He always worked. When there was no other way to get there, Daddy walked to work. He would get up early in the morning and start out on his 30-mile journey. To Daddy, it was not heroic. It was simple. He had children to provide for.

Daddy changed jobs almost as often as we moved. He refused to kowtow and didn't hesitate to speak his mind. He was known for telling off supervisors, but it never took him more than a few days to find a new and better job because Daddy was smart. When I look back at the skills and knowledge that Daddy had, I am amazed, proud and grateful to have inherited a portion of his intelligence. I often say that if Daddy had had more than a third grade education, he would have ruled the world.

It was not unusual for the employers whom he had walked out on to call him and say, "Lee, why don't you come on back to work?" These men seemed to like Daddy. In a way, it seemed as if they enjoyed hearing the naked truth, or maybe they just appreciated a little backbone in a Black man. In either case, Daddy always worked.

Still, money was always tight. But Daddy was imaginative, creative and extremely resourceful at making ends meet. We were usually able to live in a decent house and wear decent clothing. He didn't allow us to go hungry. He grew vegetables, hunted and fished. We ate loads of vegetables and every wildlife imaginable: raccoons, birds, possums, squirrels and rabbits. When Daddy would go fishing, we would pray that he wouldn't catch anything because we children didn't like to clean fish. But God knew we needed food, and Daddy would come back with buckets of fish almost every time.

Daddy was infinitely resourceful in so many areas. He found ways to add fun and excitement to our lives. He took us places on weekends. He showed us that there was another world out there and that it was open to us.

Daddy, Can I Tell You Something?

Daddy thought school was important, and he seldom missed a parent meeting or parent-teacher conference. Once when I complained to him that I thought I might miss something while sitting in the back of the class, he visited the teacher to ask why I wasn't sitting at the front of the classroom. Needless to say, I was moved to the front of the class the very next day.

He expected excellence from his children. I usually received all A's in school, but one grading period I received a B and Daddy asked, "Why didn't you get an A?" After that, I did.

"The more you work your mind, the less you have to work your behind," is what he used to say. Looking back, I realize that Daddy was a progressive thinker. In school, he made sure we participated in everything. If a school bus was traveling to an extra-curricular event, be it a field day, band festival, or chorus outing, one of us was bound to be on it.

As we grew older and the family's finances improved, he did not hesitate to provide us with money to attend athletic events and other social events. Daddy was a gregarious person and did not think it was excessive for us to attend every game, play or dance. During my high school years, I tried to do everything, be everything and run everything, all with Daddy's encouragement and support.

When I graduated from high school with honors, my Daddy was not deliriously happy. It was only what he expected. And when I decided to move to the city to attend college, he was not in the least upset about me moving away from home. It was what he had raised me to do. And when I left, he gave me his blessing. He said, "Remember, you're as good as anybody." And, because of the father he'd been to me, I believed it.

My Father's Daughter

Channing Godfrey Peoples

My mother had to make choices. At 24 years old, she was a wife and mother for the first time and in love with a man with a drug problem, my father, John. I guess she did all of the coping that she could in the name of love until one day she came home to find me sleeping alone in the house, my father nowhere to be found. She was without her house key and had to break a window to get to me. My father had gone to buy drugs. When he got home, she put him on the next plane back to Charleston. She was young, the same age that I am now, and I can't imagine such responsibilities. I am consumed mostly these days with "finding myself" and paying my rent.

Today, my mother and I speak very little of my father and those days. He has been a sporadic factor in my life, usually in the form of jailhouse phone calls and letters brimming with words of contrition.

My father abandoned me, but I didn't remain fatherless. My mother divorced my father and remarried when I was a year old.

Daddy, Can I Tell You Something?

My mother taught me to make the distinction between my biological father, "Daddy John," and my stepfather, "Daddy Walter." She told me I was lucky to have two daddies who loved me, and, initially, I believed that. I had "Daddy Walter" who was there all the time, and "Daddy John," a mythical creature whose phone calls and letters made him seem more like a pen pal. I don't remember the kisses that my mother says Daddy John used to plant on my face. I don't remember him bouncing me on his knees or grinning in my face the way some of my baby pictures show.

What I do remember is being happy every time I was near Daddy Walter. I remember him combing my hair when Mama got too frustrated with the thickness and gave up. I remember birthday trips to McDonald's with him. And, I remember thinking he could leave me at any time, so I was always ready to gobble up his attention like cotton candy.

I was playing in the back seat of the car when my mother told me that she and Daddy Walter were getting a divorce. I was six; I paused and kept playing. Even at six, I knew instinctively to pretend to be alright to avoid worrying my mother. When we got home, I looked around my room with its clown figurines and rainbow-colored furniture, and I saw everything for the first time. I saw my world for the first time through grown-up eyes. Daddy was leaving me and our house wouldn't be the same. I would never be the same.

I decided then that all men leave eventually. I spent my adolescent years testing Daddy Walter to see if and when he would leave for good. I would switch personalities and want him all to myself one moment, then refuse to have anything to do with him in the next. If my sister, his biological child, wanted to spend the weekend with him, I would refuse to go along to his house. It was only me or nothing. I wanted him to choose. I wanted him to prove that I was important in his life and that I wasn't disposable.

I fought Daddy Walter in every way possible. I decided to create the pain before the pain came to me. At thirteen, in an unusually bad episode of my rebellion, my mother threw her hands up and called Daddy Walter. She had had enough of me running away, flunking school and sneaking around. Daddy Walter came. He was from the old school, so he pulled off his belt and whipped me. My mother was shocked and tried to stop him, but I felt strangely vindicated by the pain. Inside, I rationalized that he loved me enough to whip me. On the surface, though, I was so angry. I wanted to hit him back. I wanted to hurt him, and I could see the pain in his eyes when I screamed out "You're not my daddy!"

I reminded Daddy Walter he wasn't my real father no matter how many dance recitals, schools functions or award ceremonies he attended. Anytime he would get strict with me, I would remind him that I was not of his bloodline. He could have sovereignty over my sister Whitney, but not me. I was so afraid of being abandoned, I preferred to think of myself as a love child with an absentee father who would ride in on a white horse and save me rather than a girl with a stepfather who loved her like she was his own.

It's funny how you remember things. I will never forget times like then when I was hurting Daddy Walter. He can't forget hurting me, either. He told me about once in the middle of his and my mom's divorce, my sister and I were visiting him on the appointed weekend. My mother called and an argument ensued. She threatened to come get us. With both my sister and me playing on the floor, he said, "You can come get Channing, but you can't get Whitney." He said that I stopped playing and asked him why my mom could come get me and not Whitney. That moment, he says, pains him until this very day.

He apologized. He told me that he just called the name of the one he could legally hold onto. He said that he had always wanted to adopt me, but my biological father, John, wouldn't allow it.

Daddy, Can I Tell You Something?

My teenage years were hard on Daddy Walter and me, but things improved after I left for college. I constantly called him for his encouragement and love. And he was there for me. I still have my moments when I think he will walk away. I still cling to him with that fear. But I feel the assurance when he says that I can always come home.

Often people are perplexed when they see pictures of us together, my vanilla-colored complexion against his chocolate-brown one. In the past, I have explained that he is not my biological father. Today, it is less easy to explain. We have formed a bond that seems so much deeper than bloodlines. He is my father, and I am his daughter. He is my best friend, and the wisest man I know. I can look at my father and see peace. Daddy Walter has made everything alright.

The Gardener

Marcia Avent

Dear Daddy,

Remember when I was a little girl and you used to untangle and comb my hair? I was so tender-headed and you were the only one in the family who could "tame" my hair. You would comb it and oil it with Wild Root hair tonic. You were a problem-solver, a patient and unselfish father. After combing my hair, you would dress me in one of those fancy little outfits you bought at one of the department stores in Louisville, Kentucky.

You were able to do everything. I watched as you painted the shabby walls of our homes. The houses took on new life as you transformed them into magical places.

I remember you as "the gardener" at our first apartment complex. You became the gardener as a means of reducing the rent for our family. I can still see that big old oak tree in the middle of the yard and how you raked and bagged autumn leaves over and over until the lawn was clear.

I remember you driving our dark blue four-door Ford, "the blue goose," around the city. On balmy summer nights, we would go to Anchorage, Kentucky, to visit a restaurant that had a long and winding gravel parking lot. You and Mom would order frog legs, French fries, cokes and beer. On other summer evenings you might just drive us to get freshly made peach ice cream from a fancy ice cream store in the Highland area. Year-round we could be seen driving up to a White Castle. I can smell and taste those little onion burgers and that ice-cold orange soda that you would step up to the window and order.

I can never forget when you decided to leave Kentucky so that I would not have to experience the injustices and indignities that our people have faced in the South. You packed Mom, Granny and me in the black and gold Mercury and drove us all the way to California. We had such a wonderful trip. It must have taken us a week or more because we took so many interesting side trips to places like "Ghost Town" and "The Painted Desert." I remember the trip well, Daddy, although I was only five or six years old.

Once we arrived in California, you tried desperately to find a job and earn a living for us. You and Mom were able to find low-paying jobs. Times were difficult, but we always had dignity and love.

You carefully calculated and calibrated my physical and spiritual journey. You taught me the value of education. You taught me the importance of having a spiritual compass in life and how to live with a spiritual core based on love.

On Saturday, July 29, 2000, about 4:30 p.m., you made your transition to the other side, after patiently and valiantly fighting lung disease. I no longer have you in the physical world, but you will abide with me in my soul for all eternity.

One Night In North Carolina

Sherland Peterson

Daddy:

Do you remember when the mortician and his wife gave me a ride home in their canary yellow Cadillac 28 years ago? I know that it was a long time ago and that memories fade and distort even the most crisp pictures, but please try to remember.

It was an uncharacteristically breezy night for July in North Carolina. The baseball game had been rained out, and I was the only kid without a ride home. Thankfully, the mortician and his wife spotted me and offered me a lift. As we drove, I chattered a mile a minute. I wanted to impress this family that handled the dead. My desire for them to like me grew more intense with each rotation of the car wheels. However, we did not have the money or the status to carry off such a feat, so I dazzled them with the farm knowledge you taught me. I spoke about growing okra, milking cows and even skinning rabbits.

I did not know then that people in the profession of handling dead folks made "normal folk" uncomfortable. All I saw was a stable family. A caring father. A happy mother. A well-adjusted son who never got left in the rain at baseball games. They were everything our family never was or could be.

When their car neared our home, my stomach tightened as the image of your fist breaking our front door window the day you lost your job streaked through my mind. Were you drunk now? Were you in the mood for a hell-raising fight?

"I don't want to take you out of your way. I'll walk the rest of the way," I begged.

"Young girls," the mortician said, "shouldn't walk at night. Bobcats are in the area."

So, with great trepidation, I allowed them to drive me home. My heart thumped hard against my rib cage as I prayed that you would be in good humor. That you wouldn't reek of your home-made moonshine.

Just as I reached the door, I turned to the old man and his wife and waved, wishing they would drive away quickly. When I touched the doorknob, you opened the door. Your body cast a looming, eerie shadow. As you stepped into the summer night, you strolled slowly toward their car, extended your right hand and thanked them for giving your little girl a ride home.

Until that night, I only saw you as an embarrassment for your drinking and fighting. You were a humiliating cross that I had to bear. That night, you proved me wrong.

Your daughter, Sherland

Good Night, Daddy

Channing Godfrey Peoples

bedtime conversations never changed
they always remained the same
Who loves you? God.
Who else loves you? You.
Good night, Daddy.
Good night, baby.
genetics, bloodlines, DNA
couldn't come between us
soul bonded
soul joined
we had love beyond likeness.
Good night, Daddy.
Good night, baby.
Who loves you? God.
Who else loves you? You.
our nightly conversations made
brown angels
cotton candy dreams
peaceful sleep
that I needed
but never had
until you.

III. How Could You Hurt Me, Daddy?

Song From the Catacombs

Cris Burks

Black Jack, Bumpy Face, Hogshead Gin,
I knew the nicknames of the booze indigenous to our table.
Maybe there was a time when somebody called you honey.
Maybe there was a time your dreams didn't come in a bottle
and your children were bruise free.
All I remember, father, is your hands sooty as chimneys
scoffing our hungry mouths,
our lives just a stroke from insanity.
All I remember, father,
is you stumbling down 36 curving steps, stumbling and
twisting your neck into eternity.
Yet, I look for you, father,
in yellowed shoe-boxes of sepia photographs
in the arms of older lovers, among the catacombs,
I look for you. Still, there is no relief.
My need for your affection still twitches in my throat.

Big City Man

Cassandra Lane

A newspaper highlighting a story on fathers is spread across my bed. I glance at the portraits of men lovingly holding their little ones and childhood memories of you flash in my mind. Pushing the paper aside, I lie down and, after all these years, allow thoughts of you to linger. My right jaw flattened against the sheet, I am surprised to feel a tear ride down my left cheek.

BIG CITY MAN

We were loving the moment. Laughing into the dark of each other's eyes. Eating mashed-up greens and cornbread with our slick fingers. Letting the dingy juice trickle down our chins. Then you walked in and took one contempt-filled look at Dena, Mama and me and yelled at us to get off our "countrified DeRidder asses and eat with forks, like civilized human beings." Dena froze.

Mama ran to the kitchen. I started trembling. My lips sealed; I dared not utter a sound, but, inside my head, I heard my five-year-old voice ring: "Daddy, why do you hate us? Huh, Daddy, why do you hate us?" I knew you despised Mama's hometown, heard you calling it "Dead" Ridder, heard you telling your friends you're a city man who just can't be tied down. You were gonna ditch this hole of a place, you promised. Write famous romance skits, conquer Hollywood.

I used to think I was the root of your discontent, that you'd never forgiven me for the time I peed in one of your new, tall-heeled disco boots. You loved those boots. I could tell. I noticed the smiles that replaced your usual scowl whenever you got decked out in your open-collar shirt, bright gold chains, tight, stretchy pants and shiny, ankle-high shoes with the big zippers on the sides. You left the three of us at home at night whenever you put on that out-fit. You secretly showed Dena and me a picture of a skinny white woman with rouge splashed on her cheeks and proudly identified her as your girlfriend. I envisioned you and that woman sliding across a dance floor, with you looking so fly and happy and free in your brand-new boots.

Never would I have messed with them. But in my dream state one night, I slipped out of bed, thinking the corner I turned led to the bathroom, thinking the wide opening on which I rested my naked, narrow behind was the commode. And so, with my eyes still closed, I let the pressure rush from me. You awakened and switched on your bedroom lamp, startling me. My eyes flew open. I drew back from the disbelieving horror in yours. You jumped up and smacked me while I was still peeing, sending my slender frame and the filled boot tumbling over onto the floor.

"Why are you always fucking up everything for me?" you yelled hoarsely, angry tears caught in your throat.

Daddy, Can I Tell You Something?

ABUSER

When Mama finally left you for good, I learned I wasn't the sole source of your problems. For the rest of our childhood and into our adulthood, Mama fed Dena and me stories of you. With the things that I remembered already planted in my mind, my hatred of you grew, and I began to believe you were the most evil man I knew. Uglier, even, than the monsters who starred in the scary movies I so loved to watch.

Mama married you against her family's will. She was 16, the youngest of her parents' eight children and the only daughter. You, at 20 and already well-traveled, represented freedom to her. After the wedding, you drove her hundreds and hundreds of miles away from the expectations of her small hometown and settled in Seattle for a while.

Mama was seven months pregnant when you pounded your heavy fists into her back. She felt me shudder in her womb. A month later, I came out shaking, she said, and the nervous condition was lasting. Sometimes when I would do something bad as a child, Mama would stop short of switching me when she saw me trembling uncontrollably, cowering in the same manner she had when she felt your rage and your fists coming down on her.

"Go somewhere and sit down," she'd spit at me, angry, but almost as shaken herself. And I would go sit down, my stomach in knots, my bones quivering like a river.

PIMP

By the second year of your marriage, you and Mama had two children. With a stay-at-home wife, you'd get dressed every morning and pretend to go to work so we'd be able to eat peanut butter sandwiches and pay the rent.

But the job thing was another one of your schemes, Mama said, and she guessed you were out running the streets instead of working, as you swore, at a drugstore. Indeed, the makings for our sandwiches would stop coming, and we'd get eviction notices plastered on the front door of whatever apartment that we happened to be living in. You'd rush Mama to pack our bags, and we'd steal away in the middle of the night to another city in another state, until finally we landed right back in DeRidder, where we could at least get greens and cornbread from Papa and Grandmama.

You blamed Mama for our poverty. Tried to force her to sleep with your friends for money, then berated her for being a "simpleminded Plain Jane" when she called you crazy and refused. How could you do that?

KIDNAPPER

Once, Mama gathered us up and the three of us moved into her parents' home. We were safe from you there (Papa had threatened you with an iron chair). Mama started her first job. The fact that she was doing fine without you while your life had taken a turn for the worst pissed you off immensely.

You dropped by to see us one day, telling her that you wanted to take your daughters out for ice cream and shopping. Instead, you kidnapped us. You took us across the Louisiana-Texas border and dumped us off at your mother's house in Beaumont. Mama stopped sleeping and eating and stayed by the phone, wondering if we were alright, wondering if we were alive. When you finally called, you rang her from a pay phone, figuring the cops were tapping the lines. When Mama answered, you didn't say anything. You just pressed our screaming mouths to the receiver and hung up. Weeks passed before your mother brought us back to DeRidder, dropped us off at a supermarket and called Mama to come pick up her daughters.

You and Mama got back together that time. But when she left you a few months later, you knew she wasn't coming back. You

Daddy, Can I Tell You Something?

sensed her determination in the way she stuffed our few clothes and toys into trash bags and slung them in the backseat of the blue Buick she'd borrowed from Papa. On one of her trips to the car, you locked Dena and me inside the little yellow-framed white house on Branch Street with you and one of your so-called friends. The tall, menacing man stood over us with a long, leather belt. On her way back into the house, Mama heard us hollering. She tried to get in through the door, then ran to one of the wood-pane windows and succeeded in opening it and sticking her head in before you rushed over and let the window slide down. She barely escaped the beheading.

Through the window, I saw the pain on Mama's 24-year-old face, saw the silver that had started multiplying in her hair during her eight-year hell with you. You and your friend carried us to his car, fighting off Mama's attempts to grab us. Somehow, Mama got Dena, but you threw me into the back seat and started the ignition. Mama was hanging on to the door of the car when you pressed the accelerator hard. Through the back window, I saw her body rolling on the ground, rolling dangerously close to the mouth of a deep, concrete-filled ditch. She lived, I discovered several hours later when you gave me back to her.

That night, a friend told Mama, you threw a party in the house we used to share with you. You drank and smoked and carried on about how thrilled you were that we were gone. You danced long and hard with some street woman who later stabbed you with an ice pick. You survived that and more, though. You were destined, you said, to make the big time, to be somebody.

Kidnapper. Abuser. Compulsive liar. Con artist. Convict. You were all those and none of what you promised you'd be: somebody special, somebody great. And yet, after all those stories, Dena and I wanted to know if horror was all there was to our father. We were teenagers when we visited you on our own for the first time. "Go ahead," Mama said, fear and hurt under her tough tone. "Go on and let that man fill you with his fantasies and lies."

Through older eyes, I realized Beaumont is not the big city you promised you'd wind up in. It's the medium-sized town in which you grew up with a houseful of siblings and responsibilities. You and your second, more worldly wife had a new home on a street called Sunnydale. Inside, your place was decorated with plush carpet, animal-print throws and brass statues. As Dena and I crossed the threshold, you turned with a grin to see our eyes widen. I was impressed but hoped my face revealed instead the disgust I felt that you were living this lavishly when we'd been living all those years in Grandmama's old and decaying house without one cent from you.

In the garage of your home were electronics and appliances of all kinds, things you said you repaired and sold for a living, but Mama figured it was some sort of cover-up for one of your latest scams. It was true you had been in and out of jail for your illegal get-rich scams. But pointing to your white pick-up truck with "Don's TV Repair and Sales" painted on the side, you bragged that at least you don't "work for the man."

You showed us a videotape of you on stage at a talent show, trying to crack up the audience with a stand-up act full of clichés. Guffawing at your own jokes, you seemed oblivious to the quiet in the packed auditorium, even to the embarrassment on the faces in your living room.

Three years ago, I was passing through Beaumont on my way to a bigger city, and I stopped by to see you. At 25, I was writing for a major metropolitan newspaper. You boasted loudly to the rest of your guests that I got my gift from you. You rushed out of the room and returned with shoe boxes of scripts you'd written. One "masterpiece" would be turned into a movie, you claimed, the glitter in your eyes leading me to think you believed your own lies. "I'm gonna make it, baby, you'll see. Your Daddy's gonna make it," you said to me. The folk in your small audience, which also included your second wife and your sister, all had heard your pathetic spiel before. We didn't look at your face. We looked at each other, passing a silent "Yeah, right."

A second later, though, I caught a glimpse of the scribbled-on scraps of paper shaking in your hand and, for the first time, I pictured you as a young man filled with hope for a better life. For the first time, you looked vulnerable to me.

Before I started kindergarten, before I learned to spell my name correctly, you taught me how to draw. You'd start me off tracing comic strip characters until I could create, freehand, Snoopy's nose just so. It wasn't particularly fun. In fact, it was quite meticulous: Draw a line. Erase it. Start over. My neck and fingers would ache, but, afraid to complain, I would begin to savor the softness of your breath behind my ear, the warmth of your large fingers closing over my tiny ones.

When I look back on those moments now, I realize why they resurrect a tenderness in me, despite that you hurled harsh words at me when my erasing tore the delicate paper. You were more interested in the mechanics of the drawings than me. Still, I don't totally regret those moments because you were giving me, in your own way, a slice of advice about life: that to produce art is living. The only way to live, really. And that the only way to be an artist is to be dedicated to hard work, no matter how tedious, no matter how unglamorous. I do regret that you didn't succeed.

Even from your newest home, a prison cell, you continue to dream. You've written two novels, you said in a letter. Some poetry, too. This time, you wrote, your plans to make something of yourself are as "solid as black and white." "I wish to God I was free," you wrote. "I have a right to live my life." I can almost see you pounding the cell wall with your fist.

"You're just like your Daddy," my friend Patrick joked after I told him stories of your wild aspirations. I let out a surprised yelp, but deep down I knew what he meant. I had just quit my job at the newspaper. While it gave me financial stability, I was miserable because I found my environment stifling, my writing basically restricted to reports on road projects and school board meetings. Eventually, I mustered up the courage to parole myself from my prison. Some people think I am crazy for leaving a good paying position to pursue my dreams of writing. They demand to know what I am going to do with my life now. When I am going to have children. I remember how we used to look at you whenever someone squirms now and avoids my eyes as I talk about my goals to write books, to be an entrepreneur, to see the world.

On Father's Day, I lie down across my bed and think about the similarities between us. It is true that, like you, I am breaking from tradition. Like you, I am daring to pursue my dreams. Yet, I couldn't feel this part of you that is in me until I took that leap, until I freed myself from debilitating self-doubt, until I was able to love all of me, until I stopped hating you.

Six years ago, I wrote a letter to you, but I am glad that I never mailed it. At that time, I despised you for the impact your negligence, abuse and disappointments had on me, on Mama, and Dena. While I no longer hate you, I will never forget my past with you. As I, in a sense, follow in your footsteps, I pledge to be other things that you were not: honest, loving, sensitive and responsible.

Despite my recently attained positive outlook, though, everyday I confront my deep fear of failing and crashing as hard as you did. Then, I sit down at my computer and begin to sketch scenes and feelings with my keyboard, typing, deleting, and re-typing the lines, performing the tedious task of being a writer.

Hoping that someday I will be somebody great.

Your Daughter, Cassandra

I Don't Know Why My Daddy Was So Mean

Eva Belle Mathis (Mitchell)

(Recorded November 20, 2000 at the age of 84)

My father was a very handsome man, tall, at least six feet, very dark. He looked as if he had some Indian in him and from his demeanor and types of things about him, I would say he did. He was a man who could do almost anything and what I mean by anything is from gardening to building to carving to drawing pictures, he was even good at doing cement work.

We lived in Georgia. I can't tell you what year he was born, exactly, but he never had any education. The only thing he could do is print his name. But if you wanted him to build something or do any of those kind of things, the man was a marvel.

He was very civic-minded too. Wherever there was a path that the Negro women had to cross and the walk wasn't very well taken care of, he would make them bridges to go across so they wouldn't have to step in the mud or the stream. He was that type of person.

But on the other side, with his children, he was so mean. I don't know why this was so. I don't know if it was because he wanted us to grow up to be god-fearing people or good people or whatever you might say, but he was so mean to us. He beat us from sunup to sundown, and talked mean all the time.

My father had two sons, one was named Robert and the other was named Horace. I remember Horace very much. When I went to live with my father, I was about four years old and Horace was eighteen. And I can remember Horace doing something that my father didn't like. My father just didn't like it. He beat the boy, and he beat him so bad that the boy ran away. My father never saw him again. But he grew up to be one of the best dancers, he and his brother, in Atlanta, Georgia. They danced at the 81 Theatre and from the 81 Theatre they went to New York. I saw him once in New York, but I don't know what has happened to him now. That hurts me.

My mother died when I was four. I remember her. I was little when she died, but I remember her. I remember one incident especially, with my father. I remember one day my father came to see my mother. And he hit my mother. What in the world he hit my mother for, I don't know. My mother had been in the house all day with me, but I think he was very jealous. They say that she was a very beautiful woman. I can't remember what my mother looked like because I was so small when she died. But like I said, I can remember him hitting her and I ran into him like I was a little chicken and I said, "I'll kill you, I'll kill you, I'll kill you." My father stopped and looked at me. I can remember how hard he looked at me. And I think I was the only one of his kids who could speak to him that way. But I said things in such a way that I meant it. And I meant that I would kill him for hitting my mother.

I don't know what she died from, but when she knew she was dying, she called our stepmother Tish over to ask her if she would raise us. Now, when me and my sister were born, Tish was my father's wife and my mother was his other woman. My father had many women, and they knew about each other. But if somebody needed food or help with their children or any other help, they took care of each other. That's the way it was then. That's the way Negro women were with each other. So, my mother said please take them and raise them for me. Tish said yes she would take my sister Melissa and me, but she couldn't take the baby because she never had any children of her own. I missed my mother terribly, but my sister and I couldn't have had a better stepmother. My father didn't want us, he said no, but Tish put her foot down that we were coming to live with them.

So my father took us in, and he and Tish provided everything for us. We had a beautiful home with beautiful groves of fruit trees, and on the side of the fruit trees, my father raised a lot of beautiful ears of corn and other things. We had this one tree that I didn't know what to call as a kid. I only learned after I was grown. My father put a plum and a peach together and got what we call a nectarine. The limbs on the tree were just hanging with fruit. That's the first nectarine that we ever tasted.

He had one of the most beautiful gardens you've ever seen. We would have spinach, string beans, beets, small onions. He would have little patches all around the neighborhood on land where a house had been torn down. And he would grow the most beautiful watermelons. They would be so big and so sweet. You couldn't bring them home in your arms, so we rolled them home in wheelbarrows. And I can remember how he planted them. He would put the little seeds in sweet milk and sugar and then plant them. I can taste today how sweet those melons would be.

We came up very poor, but we didn't know what it was to have leaking roofs or a place where it wasn't nice to live. He built houses, and he could cover a barn or cover a home. There was a family that had a home that was very high up on the road. And my brother-in-law was afraid to go up there on that roof. And my father said, "Aren't you a man? If you're a man come on up here and help me." He was so frightened, but he couldn't let my father know, so he went on up. He said, "How in the world does your Dad manage to do that?" I didn't know, but I knew my father wasn't afraid of anything.

How Could You Hurt Me, Daddy?

He could build anything anyone wanted to be built. All you had to do was tell him how many feet, how wide, or how long you wanted it built, and my Daddy would build it for you. He built a lot of things for whites because Negroes didn't have too much money at that time. This was during the Depression era. Once a man had a grocery store, but his refrigerator would break and all his fresh meat would just be ruined. He had engineers come from Atlanta to fix the refrigerator. One came, but the man still lost his food. So, he called my father and asked if there was anything he could do. My father said yes. My father put cross-ties like you see on the railroad under the refrigerator and built a new floor on top, then he rebuilt the refrigerator. I was home a couple of years ago and that refrigerator was still being used. The man never lost any meat again.

The townspeople respected my father. If the lawyers wanted to know anything or needed some help, they would ask my father to come visit them. He would go down and they would tell my father their problems. My father would say how he would do it, and the men would always have success. He even helped doctors and was successful. I don't know how this man could do so many things without being educated. But if you want to know if I'm telling the truth, I have two people who are still alive who could tell you how my Dad could do anything.

He would cut wood in wintertime and make sure that people who didn't have any help, anybody to cut wood for them, got some wood. It didn't matter that they couldn't pay. When we killed hogs, he would tell my mother to make sure to take some to others. Our meat was always divided. That was the habit with the Negroes at that time. Whatever we had, we would share with each other.

I had a beautiful horse. This horse would let us go in and out of the trees and play. This horse, my father had raised from a colt. And my father took very good care of it. And when he went to Florida for work, he sent money back to this man to take care of the horse and feed it. But he never fed him like my father fed him or took care of him. I remember this because it was the only time I'd ever seen my father cry. My father came home, looked at the horse, and it was skin and bones because the man hadn't fed him. Even when my grandmother died, I didn't see my father cry, but he cried over the horse.

My father did these things that I've told you about and so much more, but I don't know why he was so mean to my sister Melissa and me. Maybe people say I shouldn't say anything about this, but how he would treat us! The beatings. And I remember once when I was just a little thing, he put me in a burlap sack and threw me out on the back porch. I'm telling you the truth. It made me determined to do what I wanted to do, though. I didn't care what he said or did.

Another time I can remember, he came home and stepped on my toe. I said, "Dad, you stepped on my toe." He said, "Well you oughta had your toe in your pocket." I said, "Well I'll never meet you again." I used to meet him coming home from work all the time, but I wasn't going to do it anymore. So one day, about a month later, he said, "I wish I had someone to meet me." I said, "Hmpph." Now I was just a little girl, about five or six, not any older, but I never met my father again. I never ran to meet him again. What was wrong with me, I don't know. But I grew up with the determination that no man was going to beat me or mistreat me and get away with it.

Now I think that all comes back to him treating my mother the way he did. I can remember telling him, "My mother's dead, and, if she wasn't, you wouldn't do this to me and Melissa." Oh, he was so angry he didn't know what to do. But it stopped him in his tracks.

I remember he loved to drink and he would get high. He would come home high, and I would take care of him. One day he was off drinking somewhere, and we were all in church. All of a sudden, he walked in and said to the people in the church, "I'm having some today, and I'm having some tonight." And he walked out. And his cousin who was so fond of him and loved my Dad very much, got down on the seat and hid her head. My stepmother just hung her head, she was so embarrassed. I told him then if he ever came home drunk again, I wouldn't care for him anymore. I meant it, and he knew I meant it. And I never saw him drunk like that again.

I remember one day I saw him working in the garden on a very hot day in the South. He was working in a white man's garden, and he looked so tired. I can remember I was sixteen at the time. I watched him, and I said to myself, "All of these years, you have really wanted to hurt your Dad for hurting your mother when you were a small child." Up until that time, I only had one idea in my mind as a kid: that if I ever had the chance, I'd kill him. Isn't that a horrible thing to say? And to feel? But that's the way I felt. And I'm sorry to say it, but until that age, I used to cry so hard at night. I'd hold a pillow in my arms and rock back and forth and wish for my own mother and wish my father dead. But after seeing him that day stooped over and tired working that white man's land, I didn't feel that way about my father ever again.

I left Georgia and went to Cleveland when I was 18. I never saw my father again. I didn't go to his funeral. Melissa and I were both in Cleveland, and we didn't have the money to go. But I still think about my father.

Now, I have a grandson who's doing beautiful work as a carpenter, and I know that some of the work that he's doing is because of his grandfather. He has inherited his skill. I'm very proud of him. I am very proud of all my children, for they have been the type of children who have been able to take care of themselves. My youngest son worked for the electric company for a long time and now he works for Case Western Reserve University. He's not making the money that he'd like to make but he thinks of the opportunity for his young children to go to college for free if he stays there. My daughter is retired from teaching and the children were crazy about her. The school still asks if she will come back. I always wanted to teach too, but I only went to the seventh grade. Then I got my GED in Cleveland at the Veteran's Administration. My children and grandchildren and great-grandchildren are strong. They have strengths that they got through me from my father.

I am my own woman with my own mind. I have always been like that. Even with my father. I was the only one who could get away with standing up to him. And, because of being the way I was with my father, I have always stood up for myself. Against any woman. Against any man. I didn't like the way my father treated me mean. And I decided that I wasn't going to let him or anybody else get away with that toward me. I raised my children that way. And that's the way that I have lived.

Brutality

Anonymous

I was conceived on a staircase in an abandoned building. My mother was 14 years old. My father was 18. When my mother told her parents she was pregnant, they put her in foster care. My father went about his business. He joined the military to get away from the responsibility of being a parent. My mother tried to reach him but was always put off by someone.

When my mother gave birth to me, she was told by the foster care agency that she couldn't have me until she graduated school and found a job and an apartment. It took her two years to complete these tasks. In the meantime, she visited me once a month. There really wasn't time to bond and develop a relationship with me. By the time she was ready to get me, I was walking and almost potty-trained.

My father entered the picture when I was around five years old. My cousins told me that this man was around the corner talking about seeing me and that I was his daughter. I went, and he gave me a quarter, told me he was my father and left. I never told my mother about this. I really didn't know what to make of it.

I didn't see him again for another two years. He arrived in Queens for the weekend and came over to our apartment. I was having trouble in school because I would not say the Pledge of Allegiance. He wanted to step in and defend his "daughter," but my mother wouldn't allow him to because he wasn't a father to me. He promised my mother a house in Jackson Heights and swore that he would take care of us forever. He left the very next day.

My mother and I moved to Atlanta a few years later. She started seeing a lot of different men, doing drugs and drinking. We were having serious problems. I didn't think that she loved me. I was good in school to try to get her to love me, but it didn't work. Even though I didn't know my father, I wanted him because I needed someone who would protect me and love me. I thought maybe he would, but I didn't even know where he was.

I was around 12 when I received the phone call. The man on the other end said that he was my father and that he loved me a great deal. He asked me to come live with him and make both our dreams come true. My mother wouldn't buy any food for me and was drinking heavily by then, so I thought anything would be an improvement. He said that he would have a bus ticket waiting for me at Greyhound. I stole money from my aunt for food on the bus, and I ran away. I really didn't think that my mother would mind, since I was just getting in her way.

I was so excited. I was going to North Carolina. I was going to see my father, my dad. I dreamed of running into the arms of Billy Dee Williams or Sidney Poitier or other movie stars that I just knew my father looked like. I'd seen him before, but I just couldn't place his face. I had spent so many years imagining him looking like someone beautiful and honorable, I'd blocked out what he was really like.

How Could You Hurt Me, Daddy?

When I arrived in North Carolina, I was shocked to be let off at an out of the way gas station and greeted by this tall, skinny, old-looking man. He had on polyester, striped, yellow and green pants with white platform shoes and a big brown tie. I didn't think that I looked anything like him. He was just ugly to me. We embraced and he proceeded to tell me about his wife and two children. Wow, I had a sister and brother. I obtained a father, sister and brother all in one day. He took me to meet the family. They weren't exactly thrilled to see me. His wife was upset because she had no idea that while he was dating her, he was messing with my mother. The weekend that he came to see us and made those promises to me and my mother, he had just gotten married.

My mother found out where I had gone and called him to tell him she was coming to get me. I didn't want to go, but my father said that he would stay in touch. My mother whipped my butt in front of him to show him that she still had the power. We rode all the way back to Atlanta with the windows down for her to punish me more. When we got home, she locked me in my room and left.

We argued all the time. Eventually, she called him and told him to meet her in Atlanta at the courthouse and she would turn over custody of me, so he could have me forever. I was excited. I was going to live somewhere where people loved me and would protect me. My father came to get me and we left. My mother never even said good-bye.

I was in North Carolina about two weeks when it started. My stepmother wasn't exactly happy about me being there. She said she never blamed me, but she sure did act like it. I was having trouble in school, and things were terrible at my father's house. I found out that it wasn't his house but his wife's. I also found out that he didn't like to pay bills. My stepmother left him, taking my brother and sister. And then we were all alone.

My father's father, who came over sometime, moved in after my stepmother moved out. Then he came up with the idea of a lifetime.

Daddy, Can I Tell You Something?

I was practically a woman, he said, so I should take on the responsibility of a woman. My father agreed. They made me wash, cook and clean. I remember how it started. My grandfather came into the kitchen one night and grabbed my breast. He stated that they were big and firm like my mother's at the same age. He started feeling all over me and told me not to scream because we lived in the country and no one would care anyway. I just stood there. My father came in and looked on. He didn't do or say anything, just looked.

After I fixed dinner, my father instructed me to come and sit at his feet. I did as I was told. He explained to me that I was going to take the place of his wife, totally. He put my hands on his privates and told me what he wanted me to do. His father said that I would like it and it would give me experience in how to treat a man for when I was old enough to have a boyfriend. They both took me that night. I was tied up, beaten, burned and sodomized.

The next day, I was expected to clean the house, cook food and go on as if nothing had happened. I cried and cried. I wanted to tell someone, but there was no one to tell. Plus, who was going to believe me? So, I went to school as usual, and, afternoons, I would go home and it would start all over again. There was no bathroom in the house, so I had to use the outhouse. One day, they decided that it would be fun to leave me tied up in there to see if I could scream loud enough for someone to help me. I was left there for three days. No one came.

The only reason they stopped was because my stepmother said she was returning home. They told me to get cleaned up and told me never to tell anyone because no one would believe me and no one really cared for me anyway. I didn't believe that. I figured if I could get out of that godforsaken town and state, I would find someone who would care. The next day, I managed to make a call at school to my mother's father. He cried and said that I shouldn't worry, he was coming. By this time, I found out that my father was going to jail for a hit-and-run accident. He had killed a small child.

How Could You Hurt Me, Daddy?

My grandfather arrived in North Carolina the next day and was shocked at what he saw. I had cigarette burns, rope burns and bite marks all over my body. My grandfather hugged me, brought me a clean set of clothes and food, and held me all the way to New York.

When we arrived at my grandparent's house, my grandfather called my mother and told her to come. She had moved back in with them. She came and saw me, but instead of caring about me, she got upset at her father. She said that he had no business going behind her back to get me. My grandfather told her that I was abused and probably molested. She said I had made the whole story up to get attention and there was no way that an adult, my own father and grandfather, would do that to me.

The next day, my grandfather took me to the doctor. He told my grandfather that I'd been raped and severely abused. The doctor told me that I was pregnant, but I didn't tell anyone that. I'd have an abortion. I wouldn't give birth to my father's or grandfather's baby.

The doctor said that my outer wounds would heal but that I would need a lot of counseling and whoever hurt me should be in jail. My grandfather took the report to show my mother, who looked me right in the face and called me a slut. She said that if I wasn't sleeping around with boys then none of this would have happened.

That was it for me. I figured that if my own mother didn't believe me, looking at the outer marks on me, what was the point of telling a counselor? I decided that day never to tell anyone else, never to let anyone close to me and never to ask for help again. I was taken to counselors, but I wouldn't say anything. I would just stare at the walls. I continued to stay with my grandparents and go to school. My grandfather made me feel special and loved. He always took care of my grandmother, the church, the Sunday school children and me. My mother told my grandparents that it was all a waste of time because I was trash. So, I was determined to show my grandfather that I was worthy of his love. I had an abortion, worked hard and didn't cause any trouble. He would tell me that I was more than worthy of love and that no matter what I did, he would love me.

I was settling in and trying to get better. Then one night, my mother called and said that she was going to take me out to dinner so we could talk. Even though I could tell she was high, I thought this was a chance for us to finally be mother and daughter, a chance for me to put my arms around my mother without her flinching, a chance for her to love me. She came over and my grandparents let her in. She went into the kitchen and called me. When I arrived, she held a knife to my throat and said that she was going to kill me. She had opened a window and told me to jump. I had two choices, I could jump or she would stab me to death. We fought, and I got away. I ran away.

I would call my grandparents from time to time to let them know that I was okay. I wasn't. I was selling drugs and my body, but I was alive. They tried to get me to come home, but I couldn't go back there to live. I went home once on my 15th birthday, though, and we had cheese doodles, ice cream and soda. It was a wonderful visit, until he told me that he was dying. A few months later, he did die.

I wanted to die, too, I was hurting so bad. I was pregnant, and more alone than ever, without my grandfather. I went for the most brutal punishment I could think of. I went back to North Carolina and my father. He was out of jail by then and back with his family. I called and told him that I needed to come there, and he said he would meet me at the train station.

He stashed me at his sister's house because his wife didn't want me to contaminate her daughter, as if pregnancy was contagious. He would come over to his sister's house and take me to a secluded place and have sex with me. I didn't care. I figured that this was exactly what I deserved. Until one day, he was hitting me, punching me in my stomach, and telling me that I deserved everything I got.

That day, I ran. I managed to make it to a neighbor's house down the road, and they called the sheriff. I was taken to a shelter and then ended up in foster care.

My foster father and his wife were good people. They took me to doctor appointments and fed me and treated me as their own. My foster father's family treated me just like I was his daughter. He even gave me a name, "Baby Girl," which he still calls me to this day. He was protective of his family, including me. I adored him. He was everything I could ask for in a father. He was attentive and affectionate. He would come in from work and hug me, just because. I was never so happy. We would see my real father from time to time at the grocery store or the gas station, but my foster father would just put his arm around me and tell me that it was okay. I was going to be fine. He loved me and when you love a child you don't use them for sex. He never tried anything with me.

He taught me about cars and tools. That way I wouldn't have to rely on a man to do things for me. When my son was born, he was there, smiling like a grandfather. He told everyone. He was so proud. My foster parents showed me about caring for a baby.

My foster parents tried to give me love, but I couldn't accept it. I was too screwed up inside. I ended up drinking, doing drugs, and, eventually, going to jail because of all the pain in my life.

Now, I am the mother of three children. My oldest is handicapped with cerebral palsy. I am taking care of him and fighting for custody of the other two. I am no longer taking drugs to ease the pain, nor do I drink. I have learned that there are people out there who can help. I learned that there are people you can trust. Most importantly, I learned that I was not responsible for my father's actions, his father's actions, or my mother's. They have to live with what they did to me, but I don't. I don't have to destroy myself because of what they did. I can heal, and I can live.

My Daddy's House

Veronica Velasquez

Dear Daddy,

You taught my two little brothers and me the Bible when we were just old enough to watch cartoons. As you taught and sang to us on the Sabbath, Mama used to bake bread, feather-light rolls that melted in our mouths at the dinner table, where all of us, even Grandmama, gathered every night. I remember those moments, those times.

In one of my favorite "back-in-the-day" photographs, you are holding me in your arms on the shore of Daytona Beach. You look handsome, valiant. Even as an infant, I look just like you. The same squinting, almond-shaped eyes and modest afro. The same full lips. When I grew up, Mama told stories of how she just shaped my hair into an afro, avoiding frills like bubblegum-colored barrettes and pink ribbons because my natural looked so cute. "People used to think you were a boy!" She would exclaim, laughing and shaking her head.

Our old picture albums testify to happier times. Then you went to Vietnam. While you were there, black had become beautiful, Muhammad Ali was king, Michael Jackson had unaltered hair and an unaltered nose and Ebony Magazine gave Black people images to be proud of. After Vietnam, you grasped at the fruits of Martin's and Malcolm's labor and blood. You got yourself a fine, brown-skinned woman, a college degree, a job, a three-bedroom house, a car. You decided to start your own business. You made the garage your shop instead of a family room. I loved the smell of the spray paints, the vivid blues, yellows and reds on the white butcher paper stretched out in your work space. Sometimes, from the window in the kitchen, I watched you carefully execute each stroke with your brush. I liked the black lines best. Strong, solid, dignified. You encouraged me to explore my art, only scolding me gently when I stole into the garage and took some of your best markers and pens for myself.

Remember when you gave me that neon-pink magnetic pencil case? You gave my little brother a light blue one just like it. We were maybe five and three. Distracted from reveling with him over our having our own art things, I listened to the adult voices fighting. Grandmama held a check in her hand. You yelled at her angrily. Mama was somewhere in between, more quiet. Grandmama packed up and went to live with her older sister that day. She had to. You told her to. We needed Grandmama. She took care of us while you were working because there was a new baby. But you told her to leave, and Mama was too scared to contradict your order because you were the head of the household. Mama was afraid of you.

Peace left our house when Grandmama walked out of the front door. You treated Mama badly. I remember. She had to hold her head up and hide the hurt of being psychologically and verbally abused by the husband who called her a slut as often as newlyweds say "I love you." I remember. I remember sitting in your lap choking on a can of Bluebird orange juice as you waited calmly with a young white police officer. I remember the anger and Mama crying, but I didn't really know what was going on.

Later, when I was a teenager, our next-door neighbor told me more about how you treated Mama. She told me how often she had let Grandmama use her telephone to call the police when your anger got out of control. Our neighbor was telling the truth. Embarrassed and outraged at her story of how you would badmouth Mama as the woman who "never cooked or cleaned" in front of your male customers or so-called friends, I took my own small bag and rode the bus to Grandmama's efficiency apartment. How many times as a child had I seen Mama flee the house in tears with you shouting at her, threatening her life? Too many to be able to forget.

I know you are not a monster, Daddy. The last time I remember Mama leaving us in the rain, you held the three of us in your arms and you cried with us. Less than a half hour before, Mama was screaming behind the locked bedroom door. I know it was locked because I tried it. I could see that you had your own pain. I was confused then about your outbursts and Mama's repeated running away. I never felt like ours was a stable home. Anxiety and worry cheated me out of my girlhood.

When you and Mama divorced, I experienced a guilt and sadness that I thought I'd be immune to. After all, I was twenty-one, and I had seen it coming for all those years. Mama told me she was unhappy, and your frequent absences said that you were, too. Maybe you hate her for loading what she could of her clothes and furniture into the moving van that day, but I admire her for it. She conquered her fear of your domination and your threats to shoot her and kill her. She saved herself.

As the illusion of nurturing, supportive parents faded away, I discovered the power within to name the hurts that had ravaged our home. Contempt, criticism, jealousy, perfectionism, false pride, low self-esteem. I remember those Bible stories and songs you taught me, and I learned new ones. I began to heal. Love lifted me. The Creator's grace saw me through two years of intense graduate study, and within two years, I had a master's degree, a sweet, loving husband and my first New York City apartment. Your rejection of my choices yet again, despite my efforts to reach out to you, was devastating, but my ability to recognize and to accept the truth gave me the strength to strive to be more than someone's daughter or wife. I am a woman writer. My thoughts and words are important.

The older I get, the more angry I become at the irony of Black men like you who earnestly struggle for the liberation of Black people but fall into the pattern of dominating Black women and Black children. The older I get, the more I understand the woundedness of our people. I have always loved the power of words to inspire, to teach and to heal. I know the pen is a dangerous weapon for the Black woman writer. Black men's attacks on the writing of Black women writers such as Alice Walker, Michele Wallace, bell hooks and ntozake shange have always troubled me. Our people's dirty laundry needs to be sanitized, and it seems that only when we roll up our sleeves and get to scrubbing will the job get done. How can we forgive each other, how can we be reconciled like true family if no one has the nerve to tell and hear the truth?

I have always wondered whether your father, who you spoke so little about, loved Black people, women and children. Was he a deacon in the church? A Garveyite? A Mason? Did he attend Tuskegee University or ever read Dr. Carter G. Woodson's *The Miseducation of the Negro*? Was his daddy a sharecropper, too? Did he know anyone who was lynched? Did he have dreams of going North? How did he handle living in the Jim Crow South? Did he read the Bible? Did he sing the Blues? Did he gamble? Did he beat your mother? Did he beat you? Did you ever see him cry? Did you love him? Did you hate him? Did he know?

Daddy, Can I Tell You Something?

Daddy, I know that you are only human. The truth may be too heavy, too painful for you to accept right now, but I am not afraid to forgive you and to love you in spite of yourself. God's light is within me and within you, and we will not be in the dark forever.

Your daughter and sista in struggle,

Veronica

IV. Do You Rest In Peace, Daddy?

Poppy

Lorelei Williams

Missing my father
his heavy hands
and penetrating eyes,
the way he said "tree"
when he meant "three"
like in "Turn to channel tree
or turteen. There's a show
on Jamaica or China or an opera
I want you to sit and watch with me."
The way he came in at three
in the morning
and my small body
would tremble
at the key's assault
on the double lock

Daddy, Can I Tell You Something?

and the thought of him
waking my mother from
her pretended sleep
to lay her on her back.
I don't miss that.
But I do miss the love I never gave him
when he struggled to show me love
in street junk treasure finds,
old foreign coins, a deck of royal
African cards or a Rolex
that lost its shine and didn't
keep time anymore.
I remember the birthday parties
he threw us in Harlem bars
when we were four and five,
and how I loved standing on the stools
singing "Isn't She Lovely" and "She's A Bad
Mamajama" with my sister while a man
played the bongos in the back.
How I sat on my father's lap
later as he showed me off to his friends
in a checkered dress and patent leather
Mary Janes he bought at Saks.
We watched our parents wear faces
they polished for the public
as they floated in and out
of each other's arms to the music.
I guess he loved us
but how to be sure
when my twin and I endured
screams and curses between them,
you ain't got a pot to piss in
or a window to throw it out of.

Do You Rest In Peace, Daddy?

How to forgive my mother's black eyes
or the bald spot she got
when he knocked her down
in front of our bedroom door
before we were evicted.
I really miss his singing
to Mighty Sparrow or Calypso Rose
eyes closed and light on his feet
as he twirled us to the music
even when we didn't want to dance.

Dreamcatcher

Stephanie Renee Briggs

This story was written at the suggestion of a facilitator during a "One Year To Live Workshop" for families of cancer victims. He was touched by my comment that when my father died he took most of me with him. When asked what I did for a living, I replied that I was a writer. He told me to find a way to write the story. It was a two-year process.

This piece took on new meaning this past Father's Day when an African-American woman, who was about my age, walked up to me and said that you wouldn't even know it was Father's Day in our community. She continued to express that our men just can't live up to the responsibility. I couldn't respond. I understood, but I also knew my relationship with my father was no anomaly.

Do You Rest In Peace, Daddy?

Dear Dad,

There's a chill in the air today. You know the kind that grabs hold of your skin, burning through the epidermis, leaving it open, vulnerable. You used to call it "beyond cold." The kind of cold that makes good church-going, Bible-thumping night-watchers stay home and huddle around their fireplaces.

It's New Years Eve. You didn't seem to notice what I am wearing. I always depended on you for that. You were the one who always said, "That dress sure looks like Stephanie," and it would. But that doesn't really matter right now. My cool glasses, new boots, and the fab hair cut I had to have. None of it matters now.

You are silent. This is so unlike you. Even that lip puckering, "give me a little sugah" kiss has disappeared. Now all I can do is stare out this window, searching for the paw prints of Koos Koos, our 100 pound Akita. You know, when you requested the dog's appearance at the hospital, everything stopped. I was at home scouring the kitchen floor on my knees because Mom had been obsessing about the floors all week.

"Stephanie, the floors in the kitchen are getting sticky," was Mom's non-assertive, non-aggressive manner of speaking. "Be a good girl and go home and wash them for me."

Then your son summoned me. "Bring the damn dog. I don't care about the floors. Bring the damn dog."

So I stopped everything, packed up the dog and drove like a banshee to the hospital where they wouldn't let me bring the dog in. I had to walk her around the building and bring her outside your window, so she could romp, snort, sputter and bounce on her front legs at the sound of your voice. Her paw prints hardened like fossils in the once rain-soaked red clay. Remember how we all laughed? She missed you. Well, I think all she actually longed for were those treats of smoked ham and turkey slices that inadvertently hit the floor whenever you were carving on the cutting board.

Daddy, Can I Tell You Something?

You said that you loved the view from these windows. I clearly remember you saying that several years ago. You said, "It's so nice to see the trees, to be able to see the sun set, to be thankful for another day passing." But now I'm trying to tell you about a red-bellied woodpecker I saw today, and you're not listening. Up until now, you always loved my stories. You loved the part of you that you saw in me. At least that's what you said. Now I'm trying to give you information about something that I read somewhere about how these birds like to travel alone. Are you paying attention? Why is it that all of a sudden you decide that it's time to make this trip all by yourself? When did you change so much that your journey was no longer mine? You don't talk to me anymore. And you don't listen anymore.

Well? Just say something, please. A sentence, words that will help me define who I am: your daughter, your only girl, the one you love more than life. Life.

I think you've fallen asleep. Your breathing is labored and shallow. I try to change my focus. Especially when you make that rattling sound. I try to find something productive to do like changing the signage on the information board you designed. That's a good idea. I'll pretend I'm the Black Vanna White. Turn a square, reveal a clue and win a prize. A wheel of fortune if I can answer the question, "Who and where is my father?"

The TODAY IS section of the board needs a complete overhaul, Dad. I'm going to flip the December card to reveal the mystery word—January. Pull down number 3 and the number 1 is left. I'm trying to get your attention.

The YEAR IS section reads 1995. We'll just have to change that, won't we? Flip the 5 and guess what's there? A number 6. Now for the Vanna pose, hands out, palms upward displaying yet again another mystery number. You know, Dad, you are a smart man. This is simple, 1996. Answer the next one right, and you'll win the whole kit and caboodle. Please, speak up, Dad. Answer one and I'll give you, I'll give you, I'll give you—life. I would if I could.

You are silent. You continually stare at that poster I gave you for Christmas where the boardwalk appears to take you directly to heaven. I propped it up on the windowsill so you could see it every day. That's what they suggest in the Tibetan Book of the Dead. Surround them with what they love. Now you are surrounded by hundreds of Christmas cards. Did I read them all to you? I can't remember and I'm getting more frustrated. Well, I think I'll gather these cards up now. Besides, it's almost the New Year. Out with the old, that's what they say.

Damn this tabletop Christmas tree that your "girls," your "fan club," spent hours decorating. It's always teetering on the edge of falling over whenever I walk by it to look out the window. Okay, I'm a bit jealous of the other women. What is this special dispensation you've granted them? They're not blood kin, you know. Yes, I can hear you thinking, "meow, meow, don't be so catty," and you're right. To be honest, I like the way those metallic angel strands reflect the red glow of the sunset as it pours through the window.

It's so quiet in here. I pace. I am so uncomfortable with you right now. How could you just leave me here like some orphan? Just last week you'd beckoned me to your bed by waving your finger at me to come closer, and you whispered, "There are six ceiling fans in the barn. Six ceiling fans."

I knew that, Dad. The barn in the backyard looks like a Home Depot annex. There are ceiling fans, door knobs, bathroom and kitchen fixtures, a dishwasher, stove, paint, spackle, you name it. Waiting to go into the new house that you were to build just as soon as we sold the old one.

"Hey, if we can't sell the house, we can at least open our own hardware store," you joked.

God, your foot is out from under the covers. These damn hospital beds are too short! It's been weeks since you've been able to move your legs. Months since physical therapy was needed or they even visited, except when they brought you that Christmas tree. They all miss you. Their last visit was too painful for them. It was their last visit, you know.

Your feet are so calloused, ashen, atrophied and lifeless. Your hands, too. Your hands have been changing over the past two months. I rub your hands and feet with hand cream. Trying to rub away death.

I prayed to God that I might take your place. I asked him to take my legs. To allow me to be the host of the cancer that was plaguing your body. I asked God to take my life because without you I had no reason to live. I prayed and each morning I woke whole and cancer-free.

I wish that I had created a FRIGID sign for this information board. It is definitely more than just cold this morning. You don't care, though. You're just waiting. You want me to leave. I know that. If you could speak, you'd be playing the bastard role, telling me to get back to work and to stop wasting your time and mine. Well, guess what? Work calls. The world continues to live on even as you begin your journey home, so I've said my tearful good-byes to the weekend nursing staff. All the nurses and maintenance staff are going to miss that most gracious man who chose to come to this little community hospital because it was "a nice place to die."

You look so handsome. Your nephew must have been by this week to cut that beautiful, silvery hair of yours. The sun is shining.

"Happy New Year, Dad."

"Hahhee Hu Heehr," was the guttural sound that you sang to me. You opened your eyes toward the sound of my voice and rallied one last time. Rallied as you had many times over the past few months because you were committed to making each of us feel as if our visits were important.

"Hahhee Hu Heehr."

I curse the God that allows your brain to function, and I cry out in joy and in praise of the God that allows you to speak to me one last time.

"Happy New Year, Daddy. Happy New Year."

Love, your daughter,

Stephanie

Bringing Back The Dead

Charlotte Watson Sherman

This is a beautiful place to die, Daddy. The monkshood is Fourth of July fuschia. The geese are fat and still. Ducklings nip the edges of lily pads. Lake Washington shimmers. There are crew teams on the water, two-manned canoes and, off in the distance, motorboats. The on-going stream of freeway traffic is white noise. I watch a blue bird float past on great wings of feather and light.

I close my eyes.

I take a deep breath.

I dip my chin into the blue and lower my face until it lies flat upon the water. I think of you, Daddy, floating face-down upon the waves.

They say they saw a man, confused. They say they saw a man, dazed. And then he was gone. Did the water warm you when you slipped inside? Did you think this the route back to Mama Louisa, passageway by water, dark and silent as the womb?

132

I always wanted to ask you what schizophrenia felt like, but I didn't. Your doctor told me that it's like listening to the radio with all the channels turned on, and you can't turn them off. Is that right? Is that what drove you into the stormy Seattle night? Winter had cast its heavy, dark coat over the city. Rain poured in torrents over those who had settled down along the lake for a long season's nap. You went down to the lake and then in.

"I'm a street fighter," you often said, dark eyes crinkling at the corners as you described yet another altercation with your wheel-chair-bound roommate at the long-term care facility that you would never call home.

"I'll bite and scratch, kick and claw," you said, showing a row of pink gums. You had made too many pairs of dentures disappear, so I refused to buy another.

A street fighter ready to throw a sucker punch. Memories of Joe Louis flashed in your mind. Right hook, upper-cut. But it was cata-tonic, manic-depressive, schizophrenia that finally laid you out.

I thought I'd most remember your war stories and how we'd laugh at the thought of you, seventy-five-year-old-street-fighter, struggling with roommates and attendants when you couldn't even walk the streets safely without your cane. Or, maybe the memory of rubbing psoriasis medication into the green blotches that mot-tled your butterscotch skin. "You're a good daughter," you said.

Clipping your salt and pepper hair was another memory I thought I'd cherish. Standing as close as we'd ever get in this life, stroking your face as I trimmed away the overgrown hairs from your nose and ears. I was trying to cut away the signs of mental ill-ness. Wanting to keep you handsome and sane.

Growing up, I did not believe that you were a "real father." Your illness was bigger to me than our relationship as father and daughter. You were crazy, and I couldn't look to a crazy man for protection or advice or guidance. You were an embarrassment, a shame, I did not want to love you, and I did not want your love.

Daddy, Can I Tell You Something?

And yet, there was badminton in our backyard, the hours we sat together and played checkers, or discussed race relations during a heated game of dominoes. You sent $100 per month when I was in college. In between hospital commitments, you attended my graduations, witnessed my wedding and the birth of each of my children who grew up to fear the possibility of your life becoming their own. You baked lemon cakes for me. Nobody loved me like you did.

I am not a good daughter and I am ashamed. Your love for me radiated from the core of your schizophrenic being. I have never felt as cherished or valued, and most likely I'll never feel that type of blind, loving acceptance again. I love you, Daddy. And I miss you. Forgive me for thinking of you as any less than a wonderful father.

I share your genes, and I am learning about your illness. I want to celebrate your life. I do not want to be afraid. I am learning how to swim. I practice closing my eyes, putting my face into the water and not seeing you.

Wounded

Angela Floyd

So, it was the summer after my first year of college. I got a job as a temporary community employment specialist at a job center for the retarded. Funny, because I had no sense of community. My father was dead, I hadn't spoken to my mother in a year, and I was on the run from having anything to do with anybody. I was a specialist at absolutely nothing. And of the retarded, I knew absolutely nothing and had no desire to learn. Employment I could understand, though. If they were willing to hire me on the assumption that I was smart and responsible because I was in college, I was willing to work. Plus, the whole retarded thing had a humanitarian component to it that could leave me patting myself on the back for at least a year, maybe two.

Bottom line, I didn't have anything else going for me at the time. Not because I wasn't extremely sharp, but because I was lazy. Depression-induced laziness, though, not just lazy for no reason.

Daddy, Can I Tell You Something?

There's a difference. I waited until the school year was over to even think about a job, even though I knew I didn't have any money left. Most jobs were gone, so the pickings were minimal. I just knew I needed a job that would allow me to stay inside my own head and torture myself. Watching retarded people working on an assembly line seemed fine. I didn't want to involve anybody else in my depression, and I didn't want to get mixed up with anybody else's. But then I met Dora.

Dora was at the Lakeside Adult Employment Center downtown where I was sent my first day. I'd heard at training that the place was laid back and all I'd have to do was sit and watch the retarded folks put things together. I got there a little late because I'd been up so late that I fell asleep right when I should have been getting up. Someone was waiting for me right in front of the door. Her badge said Susan. She greeted me with a cheerful "You're late, hon," but with a don't-be-late-again-or-I'll-crush-you-like-the-young-roach-you-are look in her eyes.

She was wearing a jean miniskirt with white bobby socks and white tennis shoes. Her legs were stained the color of carrots from a self-tanning job gone wrong. Her face was stained alcoholic red. She had long yellow hair strangled at the top of her head by a pink scrunchi. Her black eyeliner and red lipstick made her look like an old drag queen who drank too much and couldn't stop smiling. I touched my face just for assurance that it was doing alright.

Sheila, right?

Sheila Rhodes. Nice to meet you, I answered as I cranked my head in the direction of a room where I was sure I heard moaning.

Susan Turner. Supervisor. Are you new?

Yes, I said, thinking that she knew that I was new.

Susan led me through a large working area away from the moaning, so things were looking up. The people with my job were sitting on chairs at the ends of the tables while the workers put some kind of gadgets together. I waited for Susan to lead me to my specialist chair where I could sit and read my death books until lunch time. But at the end of the walk through the open area, we arrived at two smaller rooms.

And this is where we get off, she said stopping at the door, giving me an arthritic curtsy and waving me in.

Wait a minute. Aren't I going to work out there?

Didn't they tell you that you would be with the SPs today?

No. I wasn't told that.

You've worked with SP before, right?

No. I don't even know what that is.

It means severely profoundly retarded. You'll be fine. Frank and I are in here with you. We have a great time. Everyone here is great, she said.

Her pom-poms were somewhere nearby, stashed with her booze. I could tell she was some erratic mix of good cheer and craziness. Her overuse of the word great was one giveaway. Her vicious looks were another. I looked back at the open area longingly before I went in the SP room.

I glanced in first. A young woman with sick skin and dull black hair cut in the shape of a bowl was rocking back and forth saying repeatedly, of all things, "buffalo." A man, same skin, same hair, was leaning against the wall moaning. Another young lady, same skin, same hair, was sitting in her chair cussing relentlessly. Fuck you mama you bitch you cunt cocksucker dirty assed motherfucking ugly stupid fucking bitch. I was impressed, but a little frightened, too. I started backing out, imagining one of the many bike helmets they wore crashing into my sternum, but Susan stood behind me. I turned around to look at her, and she looked victorious.

Susan introduced me to Frank. Together, they introduced me to the workers. Rick humped the floor pretty much all day. He had so many accidents that they'd put him on a masturbation schedule. They took him to an empty padded room next door and let him take it out and go wild. Apparently, it kept him calm for a few hours. But if he did have an accident, his extra clothes were in the locker. I could help change him, but only with another male specialist in the room. No thanks, guys, I thought.

Then there was James. Black guy about six foot four. They shared with me that he had the biggest dick they'd ever seen. They told me I would see it when I changed him. But, like with Rick, I had to have a male present. Again, I thought, no thanks, guys.

There were more people in the room, but I stopped listening. Susan and Frank were both bleeding liquor through their pores. They'd apparently been in the training centers too long and forgotten what's considered inappropriate among normal people. Crazy either attracted or begot crazy, and I wasn't sure who the real freaks were anymore.

Then I met Dora. She was the only one not wearing a bike helmet and the only one who spoke to me. She said "hello," pointed to herself and said "Dora" in a froggy voice. She was small and old with short gray hair and pale wrinkled skin. She had wet, bluish-grey eyes. The skin around her mouth and eyes was crinkled. She didn't have the stupid look like the others. She looked like she had laughed. And cried. She paced in a corner, stiffly, but fast.

I slipped into what looked to be the supervisor's area in the corner. There was a cushioned bench there that made me notice that the whole room was cushioned: extra thick carpet, pillows everywhere, foam objects for toys and whatever they were working on and padded walls. The room and its inhabitants were freaking me out. But I was going to leave if anything happened. I would find a way to get by. Work any place I had to. Or drop out of school. I didn't give a fuck either way.

Frank dropped sloppily down on the bench next to me. He started tapping on his fat sunburnt hairy legs and making musical sounds with his mouth.

We really need some help here, he said. You'll probably get to stay here for the rest of the summer. I get bagels across the street every morning. I can get you one if you want. How do you like it?

Thanks, but that's alright. I usually eat something before I leave home.

What school do you go to?

Cleveland State.

Oh yeah. I went there, too. I didn't graduate though.

Oh, okay.

I'll show you the ropes around here. Anybody ever tell you you look like Halle Berry? She is so hot.

He slid closer to me.

Sheila, can you take Dora to the bathroom? It was Susan.

Sure. It's right across the way there, right? I sounded like I was eager to do it. I wasn't, but I was needing to get away from Frank before I elbowed him in the gut.

It's down the hall. And if you have any trouble just scream. Everybody is on call around here, you'll get some help right away. Dora will act like she can go in the stall by herself. But she absolutely cannot, ok? She's claustrophobic, ok? Ok?

Ok. We'll be fine.

I went to Dora. She grunted and grabbed hold of my arm. Her hands were cold and weak. She smelled like hospital. I held my breath and tried to shut out the bad memories that were trying to creep into my head as we walked to the bathroom.

Dora. I have to go to the bathroom with you, I told her as we stood outside the stall. I was trying to do a good job. I didn't want to fuck up. I didn't. I was tired of having things go wrong around me.

No, she said, folding her arms across her chest and flapping her hands around under her armpits.

Dora. I can't let you go in there by yourself, I said firmly. Again, really trying to do my job.

No.

Well, alright. I'll be right here then.

I stood outside the bathroom stall. I shouldn't have let her go in there by herself, but I really didn't want to go in there with her. She was grown. I was grown. I mean, I knew she was slow and needed help, but still. Two claustrophobics in the stall wouldn't work. I was right outside the door, and I was just going to hold it shut, not lock it.

You alright, Dora?

She grunted. I wasn't really paying too much attention. I wanted to go home. And being in the bathroom with her reminded me of helplessness and sickness and too much responsibility. My father. My mother. Me. I couldn't breathe right.

You okay, Dora? I asked again.

Then I heard a thud. I tried to open the door, but she had locked it.

Dora? What are you doing? Shit. Dora, come on out now. Please, Dora.

Another thump. She was throwing herself against the stall.

Shit. I didn't want to scream for help seeing as I had really fucked this up. But, I couldn't leave Dora to go get help.

Sheila? Susan called me. Just checking on you guys. You've been gone a while. You okay? She came in before I could answer. Oh, my god. Did you lock her in there? Susan asked while Dora was throwing herself all over the stall and screaming.

No, she locked herself in, I said, but I should have just kept my mouth shut. That's what the moment called for.

She locked herself in? You're the one in charge here, Sheila. I told you not to leave her alone in there. What were you thinking? I told you not to leave her alone. She goes crazy in small spaces. She turned back to Dora. Dora, this is Susan, hon. Open the door, okay.

Dora grunted and laughed. Susan gave me a Clint Eastwood squint. I recognized it from all the Westerns I had watched with my father growing up. I heard the standoff music and the train whistle in the distance. Me, Dora and Susan were deadlocked and only one of us could leave with our dignity intact.

She got in there and locked the door before I could stop her, I said.

Dora's not that fast.

Susan was right, but she could have cut me a fucking break. I was new. I couldn't be expected to run the place. I ran my tongue over my teeth and bit the inside of my lip. I was trying to think of something, but I couldn't find a tile to stand on and fight back. I was wrong. I didn't want to go in the bathroom with Dora. I wanted to stand outside the door and wait. I felt bad, not because of the stinking job, but because of Dora.

Okay, see if you can go under, Susan said.

What?

I said see if you can go under and make sure she's alright.

You want me to put my body down on this nasty, pissy floor, and you want me to stick my head under the stall so Dora can possibly kick me and bust my head open. Susan. Come on. I'm not doing that, but I will, however, climb on the stool and look down and see if she is okay. You keep talking to her, and I'll grab a chair.

Susan tried to eliminate me with her laser glare. I had fucked up her morning. When I left the room to take Dora to the bathroom, Susan was eating a bagel and reading Cosmopolitan. Now she was with me trying to come up with five ways to get a claustrophobic retarded woman out of a locked bathroom stall.

Dora, come out right now. You tried to trick Sheila and that wasn't nice.

I peeked over the stall.

Oh, shit.

What?

Dora spread shit all over herself and the stall, I said.

I thought that I smelled something, but I didn't want to be the one to bring up that scenario, so I kept quiet hoping to be gone before Susan got inside the stall.

Daddy, Can I Tell You Something?

Dora looked up at me. She looked sweet there, like a little kid covered in mud. I wanted to let her know everything was fine. Sometimes people need that. I smiled down at her, and she opened the door and jumped back into the corner. She looked back and forth between me and Susan.

Oh, Dora. Susan said kindly. Then she looked at me with a scowl.

Sheila, you're gonna have to clean this up. And maybe now you'll be more careful.

I'm not cleaning this up. I'm sorry this happened, but I can't clean this up, I told her.

I didn't do diseases or disease clean-up. I had spent most of the past year cleaning up after my father's cancer. That was all the blood, piss, shit and vomit that I was ever going to clean up. Well, I mean I'd do it for my father if I could have him back again, but nobody else. I started walking out, but I turned around because I heard Dora laughing.

You need to grow up, Susan said.

I did need to grow up, but without a bunch of craziness around me. I was done dealing with Susan, but I didn't want to leave Dora, so I went to another bathroom. To think.

Are you alright, Sheila? Frank called to me from the hall.

Yes, I answered weakly trying to sound like the victim, but I didn't do victim well. I was just tired.

Okay. I talked to Susan. She's not upset anymore. She was just a little frustrated. We're understaffed today. You don't have to clean up anything. It's been taken care of. Just head back to the room when you're ready.

No. I'm leaving.

Look, we really need you today. I'm asking you to stay. Leaving is not going to look good for you.

Fuck you, I thought. I passed Frank on the way out. He looked stunned, but I had to go. I just didn't do conflict. I couldn't. I walked first. Nothing was worth it anymore.

I couldn't even remember how to get home. I felt like everything around me was moving too fast, and I couldn't focus. Since the day I found out my father was sick, everything began to move too fast. Surgery, medicine, radiation, more medicine, heart attack, more medicine, another heart attack, more medicine. I cleaned up after him, bathed him, fed him, gave him pills, gave him more pills, and anything else that was called for. I kept a journal of how he was feeling. I lived his dying all day and in my dreams in the few hours of sleep I could get. I was seventeen trying to chase down his disease, capture it and save his life. I was, after all, to blame. Trying to figure out what to do now was like trying to read the writing on the side of a moving train.

I stopped at a pay phone down the block from the center. I was a wreck, staring at the phone trying to conjure up someone to call. I had two bad choices: Ian, a Jamaican guy I'd met at school. He was beautiful. English slid out of his mouth dressed in lingerie, ready for bed. He had touched me twice, just on my arm, and the warmth of his hand unnerved me. I hadn't had a chance to have sex for the first time between the cancer, my mother's lunacy, and mine. I wanted to be with him. But he wasn't the one to call. He was on the run just like me. He raised his eyebrows in suspicion if you asked him about the weather, let alone anything about himself.

The other choice was my mother. The last time we spoke was the night my father died.

I came home from work that night and went to his room. She was lying on the bed next to him. He's dead, she said. She wasn't crying. She just stared at me hard. I started to move to him, and she threw his juice container at me. She said to leave him alone. She said that he'd asked for me, and she'd reminded him that I wasn't the daughter he thought I was, that I'd always been a disappointment, that I didn't care about him because if I did I would have been there. Now she had called me a tramp, a liar, stupid, worthless, and ugly many times in my life, but this time I thought he was so sick he had surely absorbed what she said, and she'd ruined the only love I'd ever had. Right then, and still, I always wished it was her dead instead of him.

I didn't call anyone. I got on the bus, made it home and went to bed.

The phone rang around 6:30 the next morning. It was the job calling to give me my assignment, which center to go to. I didn't answer. I unplugged the phone and stayed in bed all day reading books about death, so I wouldn't forget and move on. I also had cancer books. So I would never make a mistake with someone's life again. I took the books everywhere I went. And, sometimes, while reading them, I would hold my breath and put my hand on my chest. I wanted to remember my head on my father's chest after he died. The silence in his chest was deafening. It haunted me. That silence is the only absolutely final thing in life.

I dreamed of my father that night, like always. In the dream, I hear something fall on the floor next to my bed. I lean over and my father's dead, naked body is there with his arms stiff at his sides like in the casket. I reach for him and his eyes pop open and his arm comes up toward me. Why weren't you there? He says to me. Don't you love me? Why didn't you save me? One tear stops in the middle of his cheek then his arm falls back onto the floor. I can see through his chest. It is empty, no lungs, no heart. The dream was the same as every other night, except that night, I saw Dora in the background pacing.

After the nightmare, I couldn't go back to sleep, so I started making a budget that didn't look so good. Lots of school expenses on one side. No income on the other. The phone rang at seven. I felt like I had on an ankle monitor. They asked if I could report to the Lakeside facility. I said yes. Need food. Will work.

Hey, all.

Good morning, Sheila. Frank didn't say it like he meant it. Susan didn't respond at all.

I looked around for Dora. She was in her corner smiling at me. Hey, Dora.

She grunted, still smiling.

I think she likes you, Frank said and winked at me.

I went to sit with Dora. She pointed to a picture on the windowsill next to her corner. I went over and looked at it. It was Dora with another woman. They looked alike.

Who's that, Dora? Is that your mother?

She grunted.

That's your Mom. She's pretty. You look alike. Where is she?

She hunched her shoulders.

Dora's mother's dead, Frank said.

She pointed to me.

Me? My mom? She's around. We don't look alike though. I look like my Dad. He's my favorite. He died, though. You miss your Mom?

Dora grunted.

I miss my father. He loved me so much just like I loved him. You know, you just like some people better than others, whether they're family, friends or strangers. And that's the same way other people feel about you. So it's all balanced. I was coming off quite healthy as I talked to her, although she seemed to be looking right through me at the lonely wreck I really was.

She pointed to herself.

Yes, I like you. You like me?

She smiled. And I smiled, too. I really did like her. I was drawn to her. I was interested in her, and I hadn't been interested in much of anything lately. She wasn't so painfully alive that her breathing and talking and living suffocated me the way I felt with other people. She was there and not there, just enough for me to feel comfortable with.

Over the next few weeks, we spent every day together. We played with blocks and worked on lining some boxes with

Daddy, Can I Tell You Something?

Styrofoam. We didn't talk. I didn't care, though. I didn't need to have that. My relationship with death had ripped the tongue out of my mouth, broken my teeth, gouged out my eyes, severed my nerves and knocked the hearing out of my head. I was just moving through. Me and Dora weren't about words. Our sadness was so dense, everyone left us alone.

Finally, though, I told Dora about my father. I had never talked about him before. There was never a need. At the table drinking coffee every morning with his toolbox on the chair next to him. In his recliner every night. That's the way I thought of him. I knew him by things. He was Tennessee. Red, country, fertile, dignified, sharp, graceful, beautiful, pained, indestructable. He was Cleveland. The #1 and #10 buses. St. Clair. 105th Street. The janitor at the Woodhill Projects. Eagles Grocery Store. The African Room Bar for pool and a drink. 5:30 phone call home for the grocery list. 7:00 knob shake home with the groceries. Lottery tickets. Bus passes. Bus passes with lottery number plans written on the back. The racetrack. Tools. White T-shirts. Big brown work boots. A lap for Tom and Jerry. Brandy with orange juice. Money. No money. Christmas gifts. No Christmas gifts. Kisses. Piggyback rides. Rough cheeks. Dimples. And Doral cigarettes. And Doral cigarettes. And Doral cigarettes. Then he became cancer. Then death.

I told Dora all of this and the pieces of him made me smile. But then I had to tell her how I'd killed him. I had to tell her. So, I told her how for a couple of years before he died, I knew he was sick and didn't tell anyone. I didn't tell anyone how he was holding his chest and moaning at night. I wanted to tell someone how hard he was coughing or about the blood I'd noticed in his vomit. Instead, I snuck around cleaning up after him when he got sick, watching him sleep, holding his hand when he woke up in pain, and holding a mirror over his face at night to make sure he was still breathing. He asked me not to tell, and I didn't. I fucked up. If I would have said something, I could have saved him. I just didn't think about cancer. I didn't know, Dora, I told her. I begged her for forgiveness. Somebody had to forgive me.

Dora listened. We were close inside my secret. I took her to the bathroom everyday and held the door while she went. She said her name when she was ready to come out. She wasn't afraid of the shut door, she was afraid of people like Susan and Frank shutting doors on her. Dora didn't care for their jokes and thoughtlessness. And they didn't care about her. But I did. And I would be constant for her, despite the fact that the job sucked. I wouldn't let her down.

Good morning, Dora. I meant it. I hadn't had a nightmare for the first time in a while.

She grunted. She was looking at my bag.

Want some? I asked her.

Can she have some doughnut? I asked Susan.

She sighed with irritation.

No. We don't feed them. They all have their own foods that they have to eat.

That's right, but did you see the way I asked you first, Susan? Pretty good work, right?

We don't give awards for common sense.

I made a sizzle sound at her.

Later, I was telling Dora that I thought I was ready to open up with Ian since things were going so well with her and me. She looked at me and touched my hand for a second. Then she jumped up and started pacing back and forth, muttering. I backed away.

Don't worry about Dora, Susan said. Sometimes she seems like she's communicating, but she's not. She can't. She lives inside herself. Don't let it bother you. You can't really get attached to anybody here.

I'm not attached to anybody, I said.

I pulled up to the table with my Essence magazine and read the same sentence at least fifteen times. I was having breakthrough talks with someone who can't have a relationship, who doesn't even know what a relationship is, and I was idiotic enough to expect something in return. Fuck this place and damn Dora. I stayed in the corner until lunch time.

I went to McDonald's. I needed some normalcy. I had eaten a cheeseburger and french-fries everyday since my life fell apart. Just for the order of it. It's always the same, including the bum that asked me for a quarter when I was leaving. I knew him, this was his spot and mine. I'd never spoken to him because I thought he was crazy, but he didn't look so crazy now. I had just emptied my heart to a retarded woman like she was my new best friend, like she could help me. So, why not engage him. I had no where else to go.

Why a quarter? I asked him. What exactly are you going to do with a quarter? Why does everyone ask for that amount? Why not a dollar? Or five?

I don't know, my sister. But, can I get a quarter so I can get something to eat?

See, that's what I'm talking about. What are you going to get for a quarter? McDonald's doesn't even have anything for a quarter.

My sister, are you gonna give your brother a quarter or not? He kept glancing at all the people he was missing out on begging from because he was fooling around with me. But I wouldn't set him free.

No, but you can have my french fries, I told him. I didn't really want the fries. I just wanted a cheeseburger, but I didn't feel right about buying a cheeseburger and no fries. Not that day.

I want some meat, he said.

You want meat? Alright. Let's go. I'll buy you one.

Thanks, my sister. But I can get it myself, you know what I'm saying.

I hear you, but why don't I just go with you?

My cheeseburger had expired, so I had to get a new one anyway. And I was addicted to the idiotic conversation I was having with him.

We stood in line together. I was diabolically amused. Just as I was ordering for us, a few people in line offered me some money to help pay for his meal. Maybe mine, too. I couldn't be sure what they saw when they looked at me.

You know KFC has a special going, he said. It tastes better than McDonald's anyway. And it's gentler on my stomach. I know it's too far to walk, good people, but if you give me the money, I will make the journey alone.

I'll go with you, I said.

I wasn't going. I was just fucking with him. I was on to him with his put-on sanity and reasonableness. Just like Dora.

You don't know me, he said. Then he started shouting. You can't force me to eat McDonald's. I can spend my money wherever I want to. If I want KFC, then goddamnit, that's what I'm having. CHIIIIIIIIIIICKEN!

He glided out with his head high in the air. I exchanged my cheeseburger and fries for hot ones. I walked out and chicken man was standing outside. He looked straight at me and asked me for a quarter to get something to eat. I thought it would be funny to start all over again, but I had to get back to work. I gave him a quarter and some parting words.

Crazy is everywhere my friend. I told him, wherever I go, there will be at least one nut there. Me. Wherever you go there will be at least one nut there. You. It's all balanced.

I got back to the center and there was an ambulance outside. Susan, maybe? I went inside hopeful, but no such luck. She was just as I had left her.

You're late coming back from lunch, you know, Susan said, her Cosmopolitan open on her lap. Dora had a heart attack. You missed it because you were late.

How? Where is she? Is that her in that ambulance outside?

Yeah, she's in there. But she's dead. You knew she was sick, right? Had a heart problem and a couple of other things off.

Daddy, Can I Tell You Something?

I knew. I knew that everybody was sick. I knew that everybody has a problem in their heart and a couple of other things off. We form our groups and agree to the insanities. I was done with this group, so I walked out.

I got a letter from the county a couple of days later saying resign or get fired, you choose. I resigned. After I mailed the letter to them, I went home and threw out my death books and most of my cancer books. I didn't know where I was headed, but I couldn't stay there.

I called Ian. He said he'd come by. I doubted that I'd ever talk to anybody again the way it was with Dora. But I wanted Ian. I wanted to listen to his heart beat. And I wanted him to shock me with his touch.

A Man of Peace

Mary S. Coleman

The sound of grief bounces
from every surface of the room, and I cry
over phantom chances. You didn't
know it; but my favorite color is blue.
Today it is ugly. It sickens me. This
color of peace that holds you, that
separates us, unravels my restraint.
Every swallow grows more painful as
others piece you together. I hear in
succession about the piece of you who
would give your "last dollar" to a
friend; the piece of you who loved
softball games equally as a player
or as a spectator. I hear about the faithful
husband who took in and raised
another man's child; and, people who
are strangers to me, call you
"Granddaddy." Where were you
when my children were born? Did
you even remember their names?
Peace. Everyone talks of peace. For
peace you relinquished me. For peace
you remained a stranger. As I watch
them lower you into the ground, envy
engulfs me. You left no piece for me.
You left no peace for me.

Daddy, Can I Tell You Something?

Dear Daddy,

functional love, I suppose, is nice work if you can get it. like a concrete job in michigan or a foreman's position up north. but for the rest of us it is fixed on, repaired daily, breaks down and leaves us stranded on empty shoulders. although I have read the letters you left us in whiskey ink, I still imagine you to be the son of a mississippi god, a tragic hero song crooned by gladys knight-a tangible, fallible man worthy of a little girl's love.

Zada Johnson

god of iron

a blues for my daddy
what does it mean
when Ogun is standing
behind you in the
grocery line
greenwood face
beneath a white
hard hat
just like your
old man the time
when he came
in thumb bloody
and broken
sent home half
a day with a
prescription
for pain
but says
the most outstanding
pain is building
a world for other
people's children
to enjoy

153

Daddy, Can I Tell You Something?

mariwo

mariwo ye ye ye
mariwo mariwo
mariwo ye ye ye
mariwo
the wild man
had been
a casualty
of progress
nailed to the cross
roads in a small
country town
allowed my grand
mother oshun
to lure him
from aberdeen
with her slate
gray eyes and
virgotic precision
but the city would
not honor a lesser
god of fetishes
so he fell
with his cutlass
everything in
his path
on his deathbed
he whispers *I did*
what I thought best
chants
> *thank you,*
> *forgive me*
to his own mouth's
> dismay

A Body Waits for Death

Lorelei Williams

i.
I am the son of Edna and Charles,
last of my brothers to die.
I used to be a pretty brown boy,
Mama's favorite mango.
I had more to tell.
I die with all my secrets.

ii.
Who eats my face?
What is holy?

Daddy, Can I Tell You Something?

iii.
My daughters stand in silence
by my bedside when they visit.
They hum because they cannot talk to me.
Their necks are soft, but their hands are not.
Do they know their grandma smoked a pipe
and never beat me like the others?
Fed me mangos from her same mouth:
bit the skin, sucked, and spit fruit into mine?

iv.
My liver is dripping.
I need a cigarette. I need
my legs. There is a wind
blowing through my body,
this abandoned building.
Once my flesh was sweet with seed
now I tear too easily in God's teeth.

v.
My mother loved my Scottish bones
Indian hair, African eyes
her mango baby, her best child.
She died in a burning house,
a widow smashing windows too late
cat bones in her pocket
blue house dress ablaze.
I die a beggar who drove a Cadillac,
pinned diamonds in my woman's ears,
fed my girls lobster and avocado,
ribboned the hair I loved to braid with silk,
and kept them in the house I owned.

vi.
My bones are thirsty.
They clack together
when I cross my ankles
under this chafing blanket.
I want to die right, like a man
but I cannot fix my limbs.

vii.
Will they burn or bury me?
Who will come?
Who will cry?
Will they pile my bones
like an eaten chicken,
or burn me whole?
Will they close my eyes?
My mouth before my jaw stiffens?
Will they see me in my box?
Will they sing for me? Will they pray?

viii.
I want my mother,
my mangos,
my woman.
I want my daughters, my death,
I miss my boat, my shore,
my mother's mango tree.
I die with all my secrets.

Resources

TOWARD LEARNING, HEALING, AND RENEWAL

"You ought not to attempt to cure the eyes without the head or the head without the body, so neither ought you to attempt to cure the body without the soul . . . for the part can never be well unless the whole is well." — Plato

THE SPIRITUAL

BOOKS:

The Healing Wisdom of Africa by Malidoma Patrice Some. Penguin Putnam, 1998.

Being Black: Zen and the Art of Living With Fearlessness and Grace by Angel Kyodo Williams. Viking Compass, 2000.

The Prophet by Khalil Gibran. Knopf Publishing, 1973.

Serpent in the Sky by John Anthony West. Crow Press, 1987.

The Case for Astrology by John Anthony West, et al. Penguin Books, 1977.

Souls of My Sisters written and edited by Dawn Marie Daniels and Candace Sandy. Kensington Books, 2000.

When the Drummers Were Women: A Spiritual History of Rhythm by Redmond, Layne: Three Rivers Press, 1997.

Daddy, Can I Tell You Something?

Soul Talk: The New Spirituality of African-American Women by Akasha Gloria Hull. Inner Traditions International, 2001.

Sentimental Confessions: Spiritual Narratives of Nineteenth-Century African American Women by Jocelyn Moody. University of Georgia Press, 2001.

Through the Earth Darkly: Female Spirituality in Comparative Perspectives by Jordan Paper. Continuum, 1997.

Moses and Monotheism by Sigmund Freud. Vintage Books, 1955.

Let the Circle Be Unbroken: The Implications of African Spirituality in the Diaspora by Marimba Ani, et al. Red Sea Press, 1994.

Wounds of the Spirit: Black Women, Violence and Resistance Ethics by Traci West. New York University Press, 1999.

Sisters of the Spirit: Three Black Women's Autobiographies of the Nineteenth Century (Religion in North America Series) by William L. Andrews. Indiana University Press, 1986.

Santeria: African Spirits in America by Joseph M. Murphy. Beacon Press, 1993.

Working the Spirit: Ceremonies of the African Diaspora by Joseph M. Murphy. Beacon Press, 1994.

The Handbook of Yoruba Religious Concepts by Baba Ifa Karade. Weiser Books, 1994.

Daughters of Thunder: Black Women Preachers and Their Sermons, 1850-1979 by Bettye Collier-Thomas. Jossey-Bass, 1997.

Righteous Discontent: The Women's Movement in Black Baptist Church 1880-1920 by Evelyn Brooks Higginbotham. Harvard University Press, 1994.

Black Women and Religion: A Bibliography by Marilyn Richardson. Thorndike Press, 1980.

Witnessing and Testifying: Black Women, Religion, and the Civil Rights Movement by Rosetta E. Ross. Augsburg Fortress Publishers, 2003.

MORE SPIRITUAL TEXTS:

The African Heritage Bible (Christianity)

The Holy Quran (Islam)

The Torah (Judaism)

Bhagavad Gita (Indian)

Dead Sea Scrolls (Christianity and Judaism)

The Vedas (Hinduism)

The Confucian Texts (Chinese Philosophy)

ONLINE RESOURCE: www.sacred-texts.com

THE PHYSICAL

BOOKS:

General Health:

Eating Well for Optimum Health by Andrew Weil. Quill, 2001. See also www.drweil.com.

Patti Labelle's Lite Cuisine: Over 100 Dishes With To-Die-For Taste Made With To-Live-For Recipes by Patti Labelle, et al. Gotham Books, 2003.

Low-Fat Soul by Jonell Nash. One World, 1998.

The World Beauty Book: How We Can All Look and Feel Wonderful Using the Natural Beauty Secrets of Women of Color by Jessica B. Harris. HarperCollins, 1995.

Body and Soul: The Black Women's Guide to Physical and Emotional Well-Being (A National Black Women's Health Project Book) edited by Linda Villarosa. HarperPerennial, 1994.

The Black Women's Health Book: Speaking for Ourselves edited by Evelyn White. Seal, 1994.

The Body and Abuse:

Incidents in the Life of a Slave Girl by Harriet A. Jacobs. Signet Classics, 2000.

Celia: A Slave by Melton McLaurin. University of Georgia Press, 1991.

Skin Deep, Spirit Strong: The Black Female Body in American Culture by Kimberly Wallace-Sanders. University of Michigan Press, 2003.

Chain, Chain, Change: For Black Women in Abusive Relationships edited by Evelyn White. Seal, 1995.

Violence in the Lives of Black Women: Battered, Black and Blue edited by Dr. Carolyn West. Haworth Press, 2000.

The Courage to Heal: A Guide for Women Survivors of Child Sexual Abuse by Ellen Bass, et al. Perennial, 1994.

No Secrets No Lies : How Black Families Can Heal from Sexual Abuse by Robin Stone. Broadway Books, 2004.

ORGANIZATIONS:

Black Women's Health Imperative
(formerly the National Black Womens' Health Project)
www.blackwomenshealth.org
600 Pennsylvania Avenue, SE, Suite 310
Washington, DC 20003
1-202-548-4000

Sickle Cell Disease Association of America, Inc.
www.sicklecelldisease.org
200 Corporate Pointe, Suite 495
Culver City, California 90230-8727
1-800-421-8453

Daddy, Can I Tell You Something?

National Diabetes Education Program
ndep.nih.gov
1 Diabetes Way
Bethesda, MD 20892-3600
1-800-438-5383

American Diabetes Association
www.diabetes.org
National Service Center
1701 North Beauregard Street
Alexandria, VA 22311
1-800-232-3472

Weight Control Information Network
diabetes.niddk.nih.gov/dm/pubs/africanamerican/
1 Win Way
Bethesda, MD 20892-3665
1-800-WIN-8098

Office of Minority Health Resource Center
www.omhrc.gov
P.O. Box 37337
Washington, DC 20013-7337
1-800-444-6472

National Uterine Fibroids Foundation
www.nuff.org
PO Box 9688
Colorado Springs, CO 80932-0688
1-877-553-NUFF (6833)

Black Aids Institute
www.blackaids.org
1833 W. 8th St, Suite 200 Los Angeles, CA 90057-4257
1-213-353-3610

The Celebrating Life Foundation: African American
Women Speaking Out About Breast Cancer
www.celebratinglife.org
P.O. Box 224076
Dallas, Texas 75222-4076
1-800-207-0992

Alcoholics Anonymous
www.alcoholics-anonymous.org
475 Riverside Drive, 11th Floor
New York, NY 10115
(website contains contact information for local chapters)

Al-Anon/ Alateen
www.al-anon.alateen.org
1600 Corporate Landing Parkway
Virginia Beach, VA 23454
1-757-563-1600

Narcotics Anonymous
www.na.org
World Service Office in Los Angeles
PO Box 9999
Van Nuys, California 91409
1-818-773-9999

Daddy, Can I Tell You Something?

U.S. Department of Health and Human Services
National Women's Health Information Center
www.4women.gov
1-800-994-WOMAN

American Cancer Society
www.cancer.org
1-800-ACS-2345

American Heart Association
www.americanheart.org
1-800-AHA-USA1

ONLINE INFORMATION FOR SEXUALLY TRANSMITTED DISEASES:

National Institute of Health
www.nlm.nih.gov/medlineplus/sexuallytransmitteddiseases.html

Centers for Disease Control and Prevention
http://www.cdc.gov/nchstp/dstd/dstdp.html

Planned Parenthood of America
www.plannedparenthood.org

ADDITIONAL VIOLENCE RESOURCES:

National Hotline for Domestic Violence
1-800-799-SAFE (7233)
(call 24 hours a day, 7 days a week)

National Sexual Assault Hotline
1-800-656-HOPE (4673)
(call 24 hours a day, 7 days a week)
Sponsor of hotline:
Rape, Abuse & Incest National Network
www.rainn.org
635-B Pennsylvania Ave., SE
Washington, DC 20003
1-800-656-4673

THE MENTAL

BOOKS:

Black Grief and Soul Therapy by Dr. Nicholas C. Cooper Lewter. Harriet Tubman Press, 1999.

Yesterday I Cried: Celebrating The Lessons Of Living And Loving by Iyanla Vanzant. Fireside, 2000.

Lead Me Home: An African American's Guide Through the Grief Journey by C. Brice. Avon Books, 1999.

"An Odyssey into the Abyss: Writing and Therapy Help Her Unlock Long-Buried Memories of Sexual Abuse" by Patti Doten. Boston Globe 15 July 1991: 30.

African Psychology: Toward Its Reclamation, Reascension and Revitalization by Wade Nobles. Black Family Institute Publishers, 1986.

Black Psychology by Reginald Lanier Jones. Cobb and Henry, 1991.

Daddy, Can I Tell You Something?

Counseling in African-American Communities by Lee N. June, et al. Zondervan Publishing, 2002.

Mental Health : A Challenge to the Black Community by Lawrence E Gary. Dorrance, 1978.

What the Blues is All About: Black Women Overcoming Stress and Depression by Angela Mitchell, et al. Berkeley Publishing Group, 1998.

The African Unconscious: Roots of Ancient Mysticism and Modern Psychology by Edward Bruce. Bynum Teachers College Press, 1999.

Voodoo or IQ: An Introduction to African Psychology by Clark, C. X.; McGee, D. P.; Nobles, W. & (Weems), L. X.. Journal of Black Psychology, 1(2), 9-29 (1975).

Sisters of the Yam: Black Women and Self-Recovery by bell hooks. South End Press, 1993.

Multiple Mind: Healing the Split in Psyche and World by Gretchen Sliker. Shambhala, 1992.

ORGANIZATION:

Association of Black Psychologists
www.abpsi.org
P.O. Box 55999
Washington, DC 20040-5999
202-722-0808

****
"When you know better, you do better." — Maya Angelou
****

THE INTELLECTUAL
Toward Consciousness About Our Cultural History

BOOKS:

The African Origin of Civilization: Myth or Reality by Cheikh Anta Diop. Lawrence Hill Press, 1994.

From Slavery to Freedom by John Hope Franklin and Alfred E. Moss, Jr. McGraw-Hill, Inc., 1994.

The Slave's Narrative edited by Charles Davis and Henry Louis Gates, Jr. Oxford University Press, 1985.

Slave Testimony: Two Centuries of Letters, Speeches, Interviews, and Autobiographies edited by John W. Blassingame. Louisiana State University Press, 1977.

Roll, Jordan, Roll: The World the Slaves Made by Eugene Genovese. Pantheon, 1974.

From Sunup to Sundown: The Making of the Black Community by George Rawick. Greenwood Pres, 1972.

The Autobiography of Malcolm X by Alex Haley. Grove Press, 1964.

The Souls of Black Folk by W.E.B. DuBois. Penguin Books, Ltd., 1969 (first published in 1903).

Daddy, Can I Tell You Something?

Message to the Black Man in America by Elijah Muhammad. Muhammad's Temple No. 2, 1965.

Developing Positive Self Images and Discipline in Black America by Jawanza Kunjufu. African American Images, 1987.

From the Browder File by Anthony T. Browder. The Institute of Karmic Guidance, 1989, 2000.

American Nightmare: The History of Jim Crow by Jerrold M. Packard. St. Martin's Press, 2003.

The Big White Lie: The CIA and the Cocaine/Crack Epidemic by Michael Levine and Laura Kavanau-Levine. Pub Group West, 1993.

Dark Alliance : The CIA, the Contras, and the Crack Cocaine Explosion by Gary Webb. Seven Stories Press, 1998.

Bloods: An Oral History of the Vietnam War by Black Veterans by Wallace Terry. Ballantine Books, 1989.

Should America Pay? : Slavery and the Raging Debate on Reparations by Raymond Winbush. Amistad, 2003.

The Debt: What America Owes to Blacks by Randall Robinson. Plume Books, 2001.

MOVIES:

Sankofa. Dir. by Haile Gerima. Mypheduh Films, Inc., 1993.

Roots. Story by Alex Haley. Warner Studios, 1977.

Toward Consciousness About Our Personal Histories

BOOKS:

A Comprehensive Name Index for the American Slave edited by Howard Potts. Greenwood Press, 1997.

ORGANIZATIONS:

African Ancestored Genealogy
www.afrigeneas.com
Post Office Box 4906
Blue Mountain, Alabama 36204
1-256-820-8794

U.S. National Archives & Records Administration
http://www.archives.gov/research_room/genealogy/index.html
700 Pennsylvania Avenue, NW
Washington, DC 20408
1-86-NARA-NARA (866-272-6272)

ONLINE GENEALOGY RESOURCES:

www.rootsweb.com
www.ancestry.com
www.ccharity.com
www.memory.loc.gov/ammem
   (resource for first-person slave narratives)

Daddy, Can I Tell You Something?

Toward Consciousness About Our Womanhood

NON-FICTION BOOKS:

Clotel; or, *the President's Daughter: A Narrative of Slave Life in the United States*. 1853. Collier-Macmillan, 1970.

When and Where I Enter : The Impact of Black Women on Race and Sex in America by Paula J. Giddings. Amistad Press, 1996.

FICTION BOOKS:

Their Eyes Were Watching God by Zora Neale Hurston. Perennial edition, 1998.

Thereafter Johnnie by Carolivia Herron. Random House, 1992.

Corrigedora by Gayle Jones. Beacon, 1986.

Fish Tales by Nettie Jones. Random House, 1983.

Beloved by Toni Morrison. Knopf, 1987.

The Bluest Eye by Toni Morrison. Washington Square, 1970.

For Colored Girls Who Have Considered Suicide When the Rainbow is Enuf by Ntozake Shange. Macmillan, 1977.

I Know Why the Caged Bird Sings by Maya Angelou. Bantam Books, 1978.

The Color Purple by Alice Walker. Washington Square Press, 1982.

Push by Sapphire. Knopf, 1996.

Wounded in the House of a Friend by Sonia Sanchez. Beacon Press, 1997.

COLLECTIONS:

Daughters of Africa edited by Margaret Busby. Ballantine Books, 1992.

Sisterfire edited by Charlotte Watson Sherman. HarperPerennial, 1994.

THE EDUCATIONAL

BOOKS:

Know Thyself by Naim Akbar. Mind Productions & Associates, 1998.

The Mis-Education of the Negro by Carter Woodson. Africa World Press, 1990.

Awakening the Natural Genuis of Black Children. Afrikan World Infosystems, 1992.

Learning While Black: Creating Educational Excellence for African American Children by Janice E. Hale. Johns Hopkins University Press, 2001.

Countering the Conspiracy to Destroy Black Boys by Jawanza Kunjufu. African American Images, 1990.

Daddy, Can I Tell You Something?

The African-American Teenagers Guide to Personal Growth, Health, Safety, Sex and Survival: Living and Learning in the 21st Century by Debra Harris-Johnson. Amber Books, 2001.

The Big Picture by Dr. Ben Carson. Zondervan Publishing, 2002.

Financial Aid for African Americans 2003-2005 (Serial) by Gail Ann Schlachter, et al. Reference Service Press, 2003.

ORGANIZATIONS:

Black Alliance for Educational Options (BAEO)
www.baeo.org
1710 Rhode Island Avenue NW, Suite 1200
Washington, D.C. 20036
1-202-544-9870

National Black Child Development Institute
www.nbcdi.org
1101 15th Street, NW, Suite 900
Washington, DC 20005
1-202-833-2220

Black Collegian Magazine
www.black-collegian.com

Tavis Smiley Foundation
Youth to Leaders Program
www.tavistalks.com
www.youthtoleaders.org
1-866-U-CAN-Y2L

The Tom Joyner Foundation
www.tomjoyner.com

Black Excel/ The College Help Network
www.blackexcel.org
The College Help Network
244 Fifth Avenue PMB H281
New York, New York 10001-7604
1-212-591-1936

THE FINANCIAL

BOOKS:

101 Real Money Questions: The African American Financial Question and Answer Book by Jesse B. Brown. Wiley, 2003.

In the Black: A History of African Americans on Wall Street by Gregory S. Bell. Wiley, 2001.

Cracking the Corporate Code: The Revealing Success Stories of 32 African-American Executives by Price M. Cobbs. American Management Association, 2003.

Why Should White Guys Have All the Fun?: How Reginald Lewis Created a Billion-Dollar Business Empire by Reginald F. Lewis. Wiley, 1994.

Success Runs in Our Race : The Complete Guide to Effective Networking in the Black Community by George C. Fraser. Amistad, 2004.

Black Economics: Solutions for Economic and Community Empowerment by Jawanza Kunjufu. African American Images, 2002.

Daddy, Can I Tell You Something?

Seven Habits Of Highly Effective People by Stephen R. Covey. Free Press, 1990.

Wall Street Journal Guide to Understanding Money and Investing by Kenneth M. Morris. Fireside, 1999.

Wall Street Journal Guide to Understanding Personal Finance by Kenneth M. Morris, et al. Fireside, 2000.

Money Talks: Black Finance Experts Talk to You About Money by Juliette Fairley. Wiley, 2000.

Think & Grow Rich: A Black Choice by Dennis Paul Kimbro with Napoleon Hill. Fawcett Books, 1997.

Rich Dad, Poor Dad: What the Rich Teach Their Kids About Money—That the Poor and Middle Class Do Not! by Robert T. Kiyosaki with Sharon L. Lechter. Warner Books, 2000.

ORGANIZATIONS:

National Black Business Trade Association
www.nbbta.org

The National Black Chamber of Commerce
www.NationalBCC.org
1350 Connecticut Ave. NW, Suite 405
Washington, DC 20036
1-202-466-6888

Minority Business Development Association
www.mdba.gov
Black Enterprise Magazine
www.blackenterprise.com
130 Fifth Avenue
New York, NY 10011-4399
1-212-242-8000

Federal Trade Commission
www.ftc.gov

Equifax
1-800-685-1111
www.equifax.com

Experian
1-888-EXPERIAN (397-3742)
www.experian.com

Trans Union
1-800-916-8800
www.transunion.com

ONLINE JOB RESOURCES:

www.usajobs.opm.gov
(U.S. Government's official site for jobs and employment information provided by the United States Office of Personnel Management.)

www.monster.com
(Website for worldwide job search and other job-related resources.)

****

We ourselves have to lift the level of our community, the standard of our community to a higher level, make our own society beautiful so that we will be satisfied. We've got to change our own minds about each other. We have to see each other with new eyes. We have to see each other as brothers and sisters. We have to come together with warmth so we can develop unity and harmony that's necessary to get this problem solved ourselves—Malcolm X

****

THE FAMILIAL

NON-FICTION BOOKS (FATHERS AND DAUGHTERS):

Whatever Happened to Daddy's Little Girl? by Jonetta Rose Barras. Ballantine Publishing Group, 2000.

Daughters: On Family and Fatherhood by Gerald Early. Perseus Publishing, 1994.

The Ditchdiggers Daughters: A Black Family's Astonishing Success Story by Yvonne S. Thornton and Jo Coudert. Plume Books, 1996.

Black Fatherhood II: Black Women Talk About Their Men by Earl Ofari Hutchinson, PhD. Middle Passage Press, 1994.

Fatherlessness: Its Impact on African-American Girls Emotions and Sexuality by Salina Baldwin, Albion College, Albion Michigan presented at the National Women's Studies Association Conference on June 15, 2002 in Las Vegas.

MORE NON-FICTION BOOKS (BROADER FAMILY TOPICS):

FatherSongs edited by Gloria Wade Gayles. Beacon Press, 1997.

African American Single Mothers: Understanding Their Lives and Families by Bette Dickerson. Sage Publications (Series on Race and Ethnic Relations, Vol 10), 1995.

The Warrior Method: A Parents' Guide to Rearing Healthy Black Boys by Raymond Winbush. Amistad, 2002.

Can Black Mothers Raise Our Sons? by Lawson Bush. African American Images, 1999.

Lost Fathers: The Politics of Fatherlessness in America edited by Cynthia R. Daniels. St. Martin's Press, 1998.

Black Families in White America by A. Billingsley. Anchor Books, 1968.

Black Fathers in Contemporary American Society: Strengths, Weaknesses, and Strategies for Change edited by Obie Clayton, et al. Russell Sage Foundation, 2003.

Men We Cherish: African-American Women Praise the Men in Their Lives edited by Brooke M. Stephenson. Doubleday, 1997.

Black Fathers: A Call for Healing by Kristin Clark Taylor. Doubleday, 2003.

What it Means to be Daddy: Fatherhood for Black Men Living Away from Their Children by Jennifer Hamer. Columbia University Press, 2001.

Daddy, Can I Tell You Something?

Raising Black Children: Two Leading Psychiatrists Confront the Educational, Social and Emotional Problems Facing Black Children by James Comer, MD and Alvin F. Poussaint, MD.

Becoming Dad: Black Men and the Journey to Fatherhood by Leonard Pitts. Longstreet Press, 1999.

The Negro Family: The Case for National Action. By Daniel Patrick Moynihan. Washington, DC: United States Department of Labor, 1965.

Labor of Love, Labor of Sorrow: Black Women, Work, and the Family, From Slavery to Present by Jacqueline Jones. Basic Books, 1985.

The Black Family: Past, Present, & Future edited by Lee June. Zondervan Publishing House, 1991.

Resiliency in African-American Families by Hamilton I McCubbin. Sage Publications, 1998.

Climbing Jacob's Ladder: The Enduring Legacy of African-American Families by Andrew Billingsley. Simon & Schuster.

Black Families And The Struggle For Survival by Andrew Billlingsley. Friendship Press, 1974.

The Black Family: Strengths, Self-Help, And Positive Change by Sadye Louise Logan. Westview Press, 2000.

The Strengths Of Black Families by Robert Hill. Emerson-Hall, 1971

Research on the African-American Family: A Holistic Perspective by Robert Hill. London: Auburn House.

Restoring the Village, Values, and Commitment: Solutions for the Black Family by Jawanza Kunjufu. African American Images, 1996.

ORGANIZATIONS:

Real Fathers, Real Men
www.realfathersrealmen.org
www.tomjoynerfoundation.org
Founder and President, Lacy Gray
1900 S. Michigan Avenue
Chicago, IL 60605

****
**Perhaps we shall be the teachers when it is done. Out of the depths of pain we have thought to be our sole heritage in this world-O, we know about love!—
Lorraine Hansberry**
****

Credits and Contributors

Credits

"Before I Met My Father" by Crystal Wilkinson reprinted from *Water Street* by Crystal Wilkinson. Copyright 2002 by Crystal Wilkinson. Reprinted by permission of the author and Toby Press.

Contributors

Opal Palmer Adisa writes to better understand life, to gain clarity, and to share and celebrate her continuous transformation. After many years of struggling with feelings of abandonment and tension with her father, she now enjoys a satisfying relationship with him. Adisa is a literary critic, poet, prose writer, storyteller and artist whose works have appeared in numerous journals and anthologies in the United States, London, Canada, and Jamaica. Her most recent published works include *Carribean Passion* (PeepalTree Press, 2004); *The Tongue is a Drum* (poetry/jazz CD with Devorah Major, 2002); *Leaf-of-Life* (Jukebox Press, 2000); and *It Begins With Tears* (Heinemann, 1997). In 1992, her book of poetry *Tamarind and Mango Women* won the PEN Oakland/ Josephine Miles Award. Visit Adisa's website at www.opalwriters.com.

Marcia Offut Avent resides in California. This is her first published work.

Stephanie Briggs is an assistant professor of English and Hip-Hop History at the Community College of Baltimore County. She is a contributing editor for the *Voice of the Hill* in Washington DC. Stephanie lives in Baltimore, Maryland with her cat Kati and is working on a novel.

Daddy, Can I Tell You Something?

Cris Burks received her M.F.A. from Columbia College Chicago. She is a certified Story Workshop director and Poetry Editor for *Emergence Literary Journal*. She taught fiction writing at Columbia for six years. A former creative writing teacher with the City College of Chicago Literacy Project, Cris has also served as writer-in-residence for the Chicago office of Fine Arts. Her work has appeared in numerous literary magazines. Her latest book is *SilkyDreamGirl* (Harlem Moon, 2002).

Mary Coleman is married and the mother of three sons. She currently resides in Okinawa, Japan with her Air Force husband and is seeking a bachelor's degree in accounting at the University of Maryland University College, Asian Division, at Misawa, Japan.

Sharon Dawkins resides in Bollingbrook, Illinois.

Jeannette Drake, a licensed clinical social worker, lives in Richmond, Virginia and specializes in dream and expressive work in group settings. She is the author of *Journey Within: A Healing Playbook*. Her writings have been published in *Honey Hush! An Anthology of African American Women's Humor*, *Callalloo*, *Chickenbones*, *The Sun* and other journals and magazines.

Walidah Imarisha is a poet living in Philadelphia. She authored her first chapbook entitled *children of ex-slaves: the unfinished revolution*. She attended the National Poetry Slam Competitions twice as a member of the Portland, Oregon team.

Danielle Iverson resides in New York City. She is currently pursuing a degree in fashion design from Parsons School of Design.

Tanya King resides in the Washington, D.C. area.

Cassandra Lane, born and raised in Louisiana, now lives in Los Angeles with her husband. A former newspaper journalist, she is completing her first book-length manuscript and teaching literature and writing to high school seniors. She received an M.F.A. in Creative Writing from Antioch University.

Zada Johnson is a Ph.D. student in the Department of Anthropology at the University of Chicago. She is also a lecturer at Northeastern University's Center for Inner-City Studies. Her chapbook *mississippi {r}evolutions* was a winner in the 2003 Tia Chucha Press Illinois Poet's competition.

Yetunde Lee was born and raised in Philadelphia, Pennsylvania. She has a B.A. in Literature from Westchester University. Lee has written a number of short stories and is currently at work on her first novel.

Eva Belle Mathis resides in Cleveland, Ohio.

Leila McCullough writes fiction, essays and poems. She resides in Sylvania, Georgia. This is her first published poem.

Virginia Merritt works with troubled youth in the Boston area. Her poem reflects the story of a young woman she counseled through her work. This is her first published story.

Channing Godfrey Peoples is an actress, performance poet and writer. She currently resides in Los Angeles, California.

Sherland Peterson resides in Brooklyn, New York.

Deidre Shannon resides in Decatur, Georgia.

Daddy, Can I Tell You Something?

Charlotte Watson Sherman was born and raised in Seattle, Washington. She is the author of *Killing Color* (Calyx Books, 1992), *One Dark Body* (HarperCollins, 1993), *touch* (HarperCollins, 1995), *Eli and the Swamp Man* (HarperCollins, 1996), and the editor of *Sisterfire: Black Womanist Fiction and Poetry* (HarperCollins, 1994). Her fiction and nonfiction have been published in *Essence, Ms., Parenting, American Visions* and *The Seattle Times*, as well as numerous anthologies. She maintains a website at www.charlotte-watsonsherman.com.

Shari Taylor resides in Irvington, New Jersey.

Veronica Stephens Valasquez resides in Tempe, Arizona.

Sheba White resides in Minneapolis, Minnesota.

Crystal Wilkinson is the author of two collections of short stories, *Blackberries, Blackberries* (Toby Press, 2000), named Best Debut Fiction by *Today's Librarian Magazine*, and *Water Street* (Toby Press, 2002), honored as a finalist for the United Kingdom's prestigious Orange Prize for Fiction as well as the Zora Neale Hurston/ Richard Wright Legacy Award for Fiction. She currently teaches creative writing at Indiana University's Creative Writing Program and is also a faculty member of Spalding University's M.F.A. Program in Louisville, Kentucky. Wilkinson was also the recipient of the 2002 Chaffin Award for Appalachian Literature and is a member of the writing collective, the Affrilachian Poets. She is a Kentucky native and currently resides in Bloomington, Indiana.

Lorelei Williams was born and raised in New York. She is currently the Co-Founder and Program Director of *Projeto Mentes e Portas Abertas,* a leadership and professional training program for low-income Afro-Brazilian college students in Brazil. Over the past several years, Williams has worked extensively on empowering youth in Brazil, including working as a Fulbright Scholar in Salvador in October 2002. In her spare time, she enjoys writing screenplays and poetry and has performed at several venues in New York City and internationally. She has participated in the Breadloaf Young Writer's Conference and is a past recipient of a Cave Canem fellowship. She has a B.A. in Political Science and African American Studies from Yale University and a Master's in Public Policy from Harvard's Kennedy School of Government.

About the Author

Angela Floyd was born and raised in Cleveland, Ohio. She received her B.A. in English and History from Case Western Reserve University and her J.D. from Georgetown University Law Center. She lives in Maryland with her husband and three daughters. She is currently at work on her first book of short stories.